A Verse by Verse Study Through

James

Meaghen Trent

Unless otherwise indicated, all Scripture quotations are taken from the King James Version (KJV) of the Bible.

All definitions are from the Strong's Exhaustive Concordance of the Bible

A Verse by Verse Study Through James

ISBN: 979-8-9865806-0-9

TO ORDER MATERIALS OR SCHEDULE MEETINGS

Meaghen Trent

P.O. Box 485

Bismarck, MO 63624

Find me on Facebook @meaghendtrent

Build the Wall Ministries

Nehemiah 4:17

Dedication

To My Mom, Sherry, for all the time she sacrificed to pour God's Word into my heart. From bedtime devotionals to long road trip chats, she seized every opportunity to teach me the goodness of God.

Hello!

Thank you so much for taking the time to read this daily Bible study through the book of James. I hope it blesses you to read it as much as it has blessed me to write it! I wrote this book to help Christians grow deeper in their walk with Christ. In doing so, I found myself constantly challenged by God's Word to go deeper in my walk with him as well! In my own walk with the Lord, I have struggled with committing to reading God's Word daily. Some of the obstacles I've had to overcome include developing discipline, knowing where to read, and how much to read. Once I had some ideas for a starting place, I struggled with understanding God's Word and how it applies to me right now! I've been through many of the struggles people describe with reading the Bible, too!

When I was in college to become a teacher, I had an entire class dedicated to helping kiddos overcome difficulties with reading. This became a light bulb moment for me in studying the Bible. I began playing around with different reading strategies to apply when studying the Word of God. While I do have an entire textbook full of reading strategies, the one that I have found that works the best for studying the Bible is annotations.

Now, I'm a little extreme, so I have an entire color-coded system for annotating my Bible. I use this color code system in this book to give you an idea of what that might look like if you apply it to studying your Bible independently, but please know that just like I have tweaked different reading strategies to my taste, you can do the same!

It is truly the desire of my heart to help as many people as possible, develop from retaining the Bible's milk to digesting its meat. God has so much in store for you in His Word! We call the Bible God's Word for a reason. The Bible is how God communicates his thoughts towards us, his plans for his people, his character and principles, and his expectations of us. Knowing God's Word can bring you peace during a storm and help you to stand firm in times of trouble. It can remind you of your worth when the enemy comes against you and fill your heart with hope when you're disheartened. The Bible is full of wisdom that, when applied, can help you lead a full life with less regret.

Additionally, we're living in interesting times. Many of us have heard the term "culture war" when describing the state of America today. We live in a time where words have lost their meaning. We speak of love, compassion, and truth, but these words have been turned into fluid things that can be changed on a whim. There's so much confusion about what God expects of his children amid the chaos. But the good news is that God's Word is unchanging and is just as applicable today as when it was written. We can find the path forward as we study and submit to his Word.

This may look like a culture war, but actually, it is a spiritual war. This is a spiritual war for the heart of our nation and the souls of our people. I praise God that the weapons of our warfare are not carnal but mighty through God! Nonetheless, they are still weapons, and weapons must be sharpened, tested, and then picked up and used. Our enemies are not flesh and blood but the powers of darkness operating behind the scenes. We serve a mighty God, who is capable of changing the heart of a nation, but first, the heart of the Church must change!

How do we change the heart of the Church? We bring ourselves in line with the heart of God! How do we know what is in God's heart? We read God's Word. It is a letter he's written to us expressing all that is in his heart! When we accept God's words are the unshakable standard of truth and choose to align ourselves with his Word, reading it becomes life to our flesh. Studying the Bible builds our faith and gives us strength. If Christ is our sure foundation, then time spent with the Lord in study, prayer, and worship constitute the building materials we use to create our safe harbor in the Lord for times of trouble. This refuge is not just for ourselves but to help those beaten, bruised, and left for dead by the raging storm of sin that is sweeping our nation. How can we offer them hope when there is no evidence in our lives of what the Lord has done for us?

Though we live in the midst of a great spiritual war, I take courage in the story of Nehemiah. In rebuilding the wall around Jerusalem, they were pressed by enemies. In chapter 4, we learn that every man building the wall had his load for building in one hand and a weapon in the other. That's how immediate the threat was! Likewise, we must continue to build a refuge for ourselves and others. We may have slacked off up to this point. We may not be as prepared as we ought to be. But we serve a merciful and mighty God who is a redeemer of time! He searches the earth to show Himself mighty on behalf of those with a right heart towards him. Regardless of what our lives have looked like up to this point, we can choose today to pick up our building materials and build with the Lord. We can choose today to prepare our spiritual weapons for the spirits of darkness pressing in. We start both tasks by committing to studying and submitting to God's Word.

It is a great hope of mine that this book will be a help to you as you begin that journey with Christ!

Blessings,

Meaghen

Annotating as you read

Annotating is by far one of my favorite study methods! Anytime you're reading something complex, annotations will help you clarify the meaning of the text, identify the parts you don't understand, and determine what is most important. While I learned this skill in a college English class, I have found it incredibly helpful in studying the Bible!

Essentially, annotations are just notes, graphs, and doodles written all over the margins. To keep things orderly, I have set up a color code to quickly pick out what each marking is for when rereading a part of the Bible or discussing it with a group.

In this book, I have completed most of the annotating for you! However, I will break down the way I do my annotations. That way, you can see the pattern while reading. As you study the Bible independently, please feel free to make this process your own. All our brains work a little differently, and you may find that you need to simplify or change a few things. Please, tailor it to your personal style.

Definitions

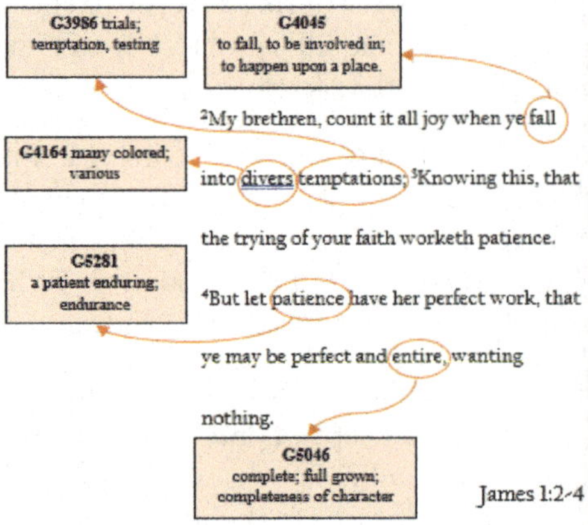

The first thing I do when reading a new text is look for words I don't know and circle those words in orange. I write the definitions off to the side.

The Bible was originally written in Greek and Hebrew. Just like many words in the English language can have multiple uses and depth to their meaning, the same is true of other languages. The translators of the Bible have worked very hard to preserve the original meaning, but I enjoy looking up the original words because sometimes it casts more light on a passage.

If you are reading an older version of the Bible, such as the King James Version, you will come across words that aren't used as commonly today. You'll want to look these up!

When looking up words, I love using Bible hub! You can either use their website or free app, and they've included all the definitions from the Strong's Exhaustive Concordance and Vines Greek and Hebrew dictionary!

For this book, I have written definitions in the margins with their Strong's reference number bolded, the definition immediately following, and word usage behind the semicolon. In a couple of places, you may see italicized words. These notate words where multiple commentaries have a different, but agreeing, opinion from Strong's.

Questions, Comments, Concerns... & Doodles

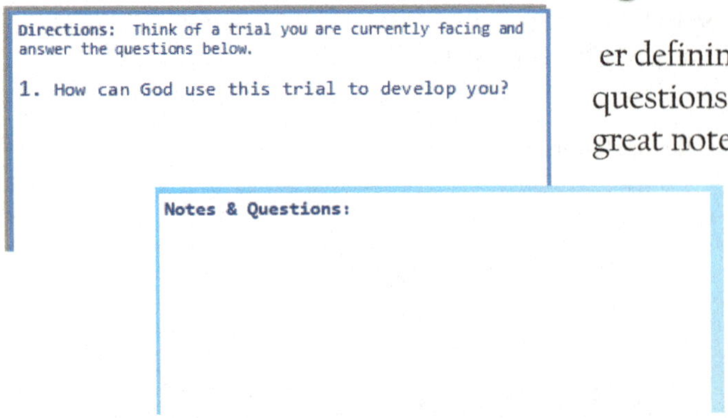

er defining the terms, I read through the text once. If I have any questions or reactions to the text, I will write those in blue. These are great notes to have when discussing the Bible with others. Sometimes, there's a complicated genealogy, many details, or many moving parts. I will create doodles on blue sticky notes and add them to my Bible for these situations!

In this study guide, you will find that all of the discussion questions are written in blue, and all of the notes sections are unlined so that you have room to doodle if needed!

Cross References

If you've ever heard people talk about the Bible, you've more than likely heard someone say that it contradicts itself. This simply is not true. The reality is scripture confirms scripture, and scripture interprets scripture. Anytime you pull out a couple of verses that seem contradictory, there is a reason. That reason is that the two verses were taken out of context!

> **Digging Deeper**
>
> Joy…
>
> **Psalm 126:1-6** Joy comes after sorrow
> **Psalm 51: 9-17** Joy comes after repentance
> **John 15:11** Joy comes with obedience
>
> Trials…
>
> **Deuteronomy 8:2-3** Trials deal with pride and show us what is in our own

The more you study the Bible, the more you will see the connections between scripture. The more connections you find between scripture, the more your understanding will grow for God, His character, His commands, His will for you, and most importantly, His unending love for you. You will start to realize that any contradictions you once believed were there do not exist at all. In the digging deeper section, you will find cross-references that I've selected to go with the daily reading, but you will likely have some of your own as well! When I find a cross reference, I note it in green!

Highlighting

Highlighting is something I do rarely and sparingly! After reading the passage, asking all my questions, thinking through all my personal commentary, and digging deeper into other areas of the Word for a better understanding, I ask myself, "Is there any verse in this section that stands out? Is there something especially helpful and encouraging here, or something I need to get through my thick skull?" If so, I'll underline it in pencil the first time through. If I come back to the passage a few months or so, and that same section stands out, THEN I whip out my handy dandy highlighter! I have not highlighted any sections of passage in these texts. I will leave that for you to do, as certain verses speak to your heart!

If/ Then Statements

While I do not use this annotation in this book, I will briefly mention that when I come to if/then, cause/effect, and wherefore/therefore statements in the Bible, I will underline one portion in pink and the other portion in purple. Then I connect the two sections with an arrow to remind myself that they go together.

WRAP

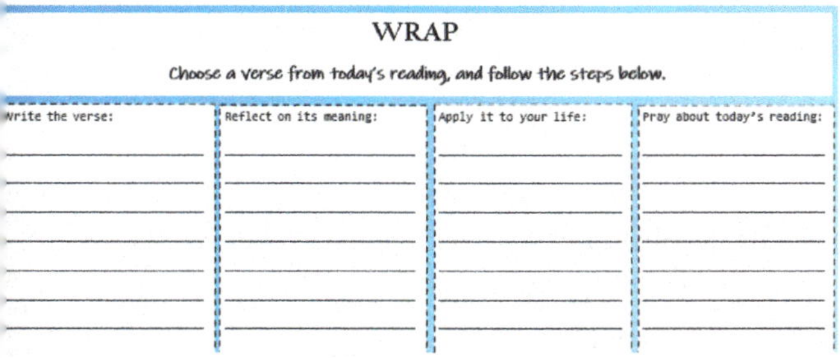

My second favorite study skill for reading the Bible is using the WRAP method! To be completely honest, I don't know precisely when or where I learned this, but I started using it sometime around middle school. In my attempts to give credit where it is due, I discovered that it is actually an ancient method of studying scripture with early catholic roots in the form of study called Lectio Divina, or divine reading.

This process is straightforward. You write a verse from the daily reading. Then you reflect on its meaning. Your reflection can be what it meant to you, an insight from the culture at the time, etc. Next, you will write down one, two, or a few ways you can apply this verse/passage to your life. Finally, you will write a prayer asking God to help you use the things you've learned from the day's reading.

Study Materials

I'm often asked what I use to study the Bible. While there are many excellent study tools, I'm going to include a list of my favorite study tools with a brief description of each one. I hope this is helpful to you as you start studying the Bible for yourself.

Tech Free Study Tools:

- **Thompson Chain Study Bible**– *great for cross-reference studies*
  - Keywords will give a cross-reference to the most recent and the next time that Word is used.
  - Key themes are identified with a code that can be looked up in the index for deeper study.
  - It offers a great variety of maps, graphics, character studies, and so much more in the back of the Bible!
- **Strong's Exhaustive Concordance with the Vines Greek and Hebrew Dictionary**
  - This concordance is excellent! It has every single Word of the KJV with every verse where that Word appears! This is a must-have tool for word studies.
  - Each English Word has a dictionary number next to it so you can get a precise definition of the Word in its original language.

Tech Tools:

- **Bible Hub (free)**
  - Access Strong's concordance and dictionaries, several commentaries, summaries, topical studies cross-references, and so much more!
  - You can read the Bible in multiple versions, and then click on the Greek/Hebrew icon and get the Strong's definitions in a click.
- **Blue Letter Bible (free)** – *Very similar to Bible Hub, except that it matches the Strong's numbers to any version of the Bible.*
- **Literal Word (free)** – *I only discovered this app in the Spring of 2022*
  - Currently, it only comes in the NASB Version
  - You can tap and hold on to any word and get the Greek/Hebrew definition, usage, and a list of the other verses in the Bible containing this Word.
- **You Version (free)**
  - You can quickly compare a verse in many versions by highlighting the verse and clicking compare.
  - Highlight verses and take digital notes as you read.
  - Has a social media aspect where you can communicate with friends about the things you're reading in the app.
  - A variety of free devotionals and study plans.
- **Dwell (paid subscription)**
  - An audible Bible app with a read-along option
  - Offers reading plans for a year and other spans of time, as well as topical selections
  - Allows you to play books, chapters, and verses on repeat.
  - Allows you to create playlists or select an already curated list
  - You can adjust the version, voice, reading speed, and background music to optimize your Bible listening experience.

Introduction to the book of James

The book of James was written as a letter to the Jewish Christians that lived abroad, meaning outside of Israel.

Who was James?

James was a first-century church leader. There are three people by the name of James mentioned in the New Testament that could be possible contenders as the author of this book: James, son of Zebedee, brother of John the Apostle; James, son of Alphaeus, one of the twelve disciples; and James, the brother our Lord Jesus Christ.

While the actual authorship of this letter is unknown, it is widely accepted that the James in question is James, the Lord's brother. We know that Jesus had four brothers, whose names are recorded in Matthew 13:55 and Mark 6:3 as James, Joses, Simon, and Judas.

In John 7:1-5, we see the brothers of Jesus mock him for performing miracles secretly early in his ministry. John 7:5 explains that they did this because they did not believe that Jesus was the Messiah during his life.

However, in Acts 1:13, we see that James and his brother Judas had joined in with the other followers of Christ in the upper room. In Paul's letter to the Galatians, he informs them that during his time in Jerusalem, he didn't see any other apostles except for James, the Lord's brother [Gal. 1:19]. This visit is also recorded in Acts 21:18. In Acts 15:13-21, we see James's leadership in action when working with other apostles to determine what laws gentile converts should be held to. Later in Jude's letter, Jude (also translated as Judas) refers to himself as the brother of James, indicating that his brother James was likely a well-known church leader.

While these scriptures do not rule out the possibility that the book of James could have been authored by James, son of Zebedee, or James, son of Alphaeus, their ministries were not recorded in the Bible to the same extent as James, the brother of our Lord. Knowing that two of Jesus's brothers' names are James and Judas and that Jude refers to himself as the brother of James makes it all more likely for him to be the author.

What is the book of James about?

Throughout the book of James, five main themes are repeated: Faithfulness in suffering, The qualities found in true religion, the qualities of false religion, warnings to the rich and favoritism shown to the rich, and disciplines for Christian living.

Why does it matter today?

The book of James is filled with wisdom to guide us in our walk with the Lord. It is sometimes referred to as the Proverbs of the New Testament. It calls us to remember that while we are saved and justified by grace through faith in Christ, we still have a responsibility in the family of believers to do the work of the Lord. We are also shown through the book of James that when we declare Christ as the Lord of our life, we're not saying, "Ok God, now you can come follow me back into my sinful life!" But we are putting down the old man and changing our ways to become more like Christ.

Final thoughts!

As we begin studying the book of James, let's look at the first verse. How does James introduce himself to his readers? He calls himself "James, a servant of God and the Lord Jesus Christ." This man, who is possibly the half-brother of Jesus, who also rose to a prominent position in the Church, could have introduced himself with all his credentials. But he didn't. In his first coming, Christ came as a humble servant. As we walk this earth, we are called to be His ambassadors to a lost and dying world. Let's remember to follow Christ as a humble servant and to be willing and yielded vessels, seeking to carry out his will on the earth more than on our own.

> 1 James, a servant of God and of the Lord Jesus Christ, to the twelve tribes which are scattered abroad, greeting.
>
> James 1:1

Day 1

G3986 trials; temptation, testing

G4045 to fall, to be involved in; to happen upon a place.

[2]My brethren, count it all joy when ye fall
into divers temptations; [3]Knowing this, that
the trying of your faith worketh patience.
[4]But let patience have her perfect work, that
ye may be perfect and entire, wanting
nothing.

G4164 many colored; various

G5281 a patient enduring; endurance

G5046 complete; full grown; completeness of character

James 1:2-4

Directions: Think of a trial you are currently facing and answer the questions below.

1. How can God use this trial to develop you?

2. What character traits are surfacing during this trial that you need to correct?

3. What can you hold onto for hope in the midst of trials?

Daily Devotional

Ruth 1-4

Naomi and Ruth were well acquainted with trials.

After the death of her husband and sons, Naomi decided to return to Bethlehem and leave her daughters-in-law behind with their families and gods to find new husbands. Ruth had other plans. She loved Naomi and refused to stay in Moab, declaring, "Where you go, I will go, and where you lodge, I will lodge. Your people shall be my people, and your God my God." [Ruth 1:16].

Stricken with grief, Naomi changed her name to Mara, meaning bitter. She blamed God for the calamity of her life, saying she left Israel full, but returned empty. Meanwhile, Ruth, a Moabite gentile, would have been shunned by the people in her new home. As widows, the two women had to provide for themselves, leading Ruth to glean the fields.

As their story unfolded, they probably felt like they were on a roller coaster. Empty, angry, abandoned, and in despair - We can all relate to at least one of these emotions.

As Ruth learned the customs of her new life and faith, she was obedient to Naomi's instruction. She faced her trial with grace, and proved herself to be a hard worker in Boaz's field.

She left Moab a pagan, but became a child of God. She had worked the field, but became its owner. She became the wife of Boaz, a mother, the Great grandmother of King David, and in the lineage of Christ. Her trial became a testimony of triumph!

Naomi found that the faithfulness of Ruth was better to her than seven sons, and found her life full once again.

The trials we face are not easy. But God has a plan to use our trials to develop us spiritually and emotionally. He wants to turn our trials into a testimony of triumph!

WRAP

Choose a verse from today's reading, and follow the steps below.

Write the verse:	Reflect on its meaning:	Apply it to your life:	Pray about today's reading:

Notes & Questions:

Today's Big Idea

Look at trials as an opportunity for development!

Digging Deeper

Joy…

Psalm 126:1-6 Joy comes after sorrow
Psalm 51: 9-17 Joy comes after repentance
John 15:11 Joy comes with obedience

Trials…

Deuteronomy 8:2-3 Trials deal with pride and show us what is in our own heart.
Romans 5:3-5 Trials produce endurance, experience, and hope.
1 Peter 4:12 Trials are a part of life
John 16:33 Trials are in the world, but Jesus overcame the world!

Spiritual Growth…

Psalm 92:12-14 Spiritual growth produces strength, fruit, and vitality in our lives
Luke 8:11-14 Parable of the Sower
Romans 10:17 Faith grows when we hear God's word.
Hebrews 5:12-14 spiritual growth is like physical growth; you start as a baby on milk.

Contentment…

Matthew 6:24-28 God provides for us.
Philippians 4:11-13 With Christ, we can be content in all situations.

Day 2

G574
simply, sincerely; graciously, bountifully

G4678
wisdom; insight, skill (human or divine), intelligence

G3679
to reproach; revile, to find fault in

5 If any of you lack wisdom, let him ask of God,
that giveth to all men liberally, and upbraideth
not; and it shall be given him. 6 But let him ask
in faith, nothing wavering. For he that
wavereth is like a wave of the sea driven with
the wind and tossed. 7 For let not that man
think that he shall receive anything of the Lord.
8 A double minded man is unstable in all his
ways.

James 1:5-8

G1252
to distinguish; to discern, doubt, hesitate, waver

G1374
Of two minds; wavering

Directions: Think of a time you faced double mindedness and complete the journal prompts below

1. What things are you relying on for your stability and fulfillment? Or what things have become idols in your life?

2. How has God shown you that he can be trusted with your faith and dependance on Him?

3. Create an action plan for dealing with one of the idols in your life.

Daily Devotional

1 Kings 3, 9, & 11; 2Chronicals 1 &7; and Ecclesiastes

In the reign of King Solomon, the Lord gave him a chance to ask for a gift. Solomon recognized that God had blessed his father David with mercy because David was devoted to the Lord [1 Kings 3:6]. Recognizing his own shortcomings, he asked God for wisdom to be able to discern between good and bad [1 Kings 3:9 & 2 Chron. 1:10]. Pleased with Solomon's request, God answered and added riches and honor to Solomon as well!

Solomon spent many years with a devoted heart toward the Lord, and God kept all of His promises to Solomon. Solomon built the Lord's temple, which was made holy by God.

Unfortunately, Solomon did not remain faithful to God. In 1 Kings 11, we read that Solomon loved many women from foreign nations, and he followed them in their worship of other gods. Wrapped up in idolatry, Solomon built a high place for an abominable god of Moab. Solomon had been warned twice to remain faithful, so because of his disobedience, Israel would be torn in two during the reign of his son.

The thing with idolatry is that it doesn't start by building a temple to another god. In Ecclesiastes, Solomon reflects on the choices of his life. Though God had blessed Solomon with divine wisdom and knowledge, as well as riches and honor, Solomon spent his life perusing fulfillment in things rather than God. He went after worldly wisdom and education, pleasure, wealth, and work. None of these things are bad in their proper places, but Solomon used things to fill a space in his life that only God could fill. God is an anchor to our soul. A close walk with him brings stability and fulfillment.

Just like Solomon, we tend to search for things to fulfill and stabilize us. When we do this, we become more unsteady than before. Whether it's a relationship, our stock portfolio, a diet, or a bingeable show with the perfect junk food, these things out of their proper place are idols. Having idols leaves us vulnerable to tricks of the devil and lead us into sinful patterns. Wavering between God and an idol will eventually lead to our destruction. A person cannot serve two masters. Eventually he will love one and hate the other. Choose today to serve God!

WRAP

Choose a verse from today's reading, and follow the steps below.

Write the verse:	Reflect on its meaning:	Apply it to your life:	Pray about today's reading:

Notes & Questions:

Today's Big Ideas

Commit to a Made-up Mind!

- Trust that God will give you wisdom in all situations
- Ask believing that he will fulfill His promises
- Stand firm in the truth of His word

Digging Deeper

Wisdom…

Proverbs 1:7 begins with fearing God
Proverbs 2:6 *comes from the Lord*
Proverbs 16:16 is better than gold
2 Timothy 3:15 is gotten through studying scripture

Having Wisdom Produces…

Proverbs 10:8 obedience to God
Proverbs 14:29 a slow temper
Ecclesiastes 1:18 much grief (recognition of the product of sin)
Ecclesiastes 7:12 life

I can trust God's Word because…

Numbers 23:19 He cannot lie
Also in Titus 1:2 & Hebrews 6:18
Deuteronomy 7:9 He is faithful and keeps his promises
Deuteronomy 32:4 He is just and right

God's word…

Psalm 119:11 keeps us from sin, when applied
Psalm 119:89-91 is eternal
Psalm 119:160 is truth
Psalm 138:2 has been exalted by Him above His own name
Jeremiah 15:16 is food for the soul and joy to the heart
Luke 11:28 is a blessing to those that keep it

Day 3

G5011
low lying, lowly, lowly in spirit; humble, lowly in position or spirit, in good sense

G4145
Wealthy; rich, abounding,

G5311
height; dignity, eminence

9 Let the brother of low degree rejoice in that he
is exalted: 10 But the rich, in that he is made
low because as the flower of the grass he shall
pass away. 11 For the sun is no sooner risen with
a burning heat, but it withereth the grass, and
the flower thereof falleth, and the grace of the
fashion of it perisheth: so also shall the rich man
fade away in his ways.

G5014
low estate, humiliation; abased in spirit, low condition in circumstances

G4197
a journey; pursuit, undertaking, progress

James 1:9-11

Directions: Answer the questions below

1. What hopes or promises are you believing to see fulfilled in your future?

2. What current character traits could be problematic if this hope/ promise were to come to be right now?

3. What can you do to honor God while you wait on your hopes or his promise?

Daily Devotional

1 Samuel 24

After David killed Goliath, he gained notoriety among the people of Israel. David continued to show himself to be a strong and capable warrior, which increased Saul's jealousy. By Chapter 19 of 1 Samuel, Saul had resolved to kill David, and began hunting him down.

While David was on the run from King Saul, he came to a cave where he could hide. It just so happened that Saul and his hunting party came to the same cave to rest. Those with David encouraged him to kill Saul while he had the chance. Even though Saul had angered God and been told that he would soon lose his kingship [1 Samuel 15 & 16], David could not bring himself to kill Saul because he was the anointed King of Israel, and he could not do harm against his master.

Instead, David cut off a piece of Saul's robe. When Saul and his men arose and went on their way, David ran after them. He confronted Saul and showed him the piece of his robe that had been torn away. He let Saul know that he had no intentions of killing Saul, even though Saul wanted to kill him.

David and Saul would continue to have problems for many years, before his eventual death and David ascending the throne as King. David, a humble and God-fearing man would be exalted by God, while Saul, choosing to live in unrepentance towards the Lord, would lose his position and die.

Sometimes in life there is a lot of space between the promise and its fulfillment. We need that space to mature in the Lord. Had David killed Saul in that cave, I don't think too many people would have held it against him. However, David may not have become king right away, or may not have had the maturity to handle the responsibility. There were many other events that would transpire in the years to come that made David's ascension to the throne more fitting at it's appropriate time.

Letting Saul live was also a crucial point in David's story. It set him apart as a man that followed the leading of the Lord, and Saul himself recognized in that moment that David would one day be King of Israel. This set a stark contrast between Saul's impulsivity and David's desire to please the Lord.

Material wealth comes and goes, but being rooted in the Lord is enduring. Proverbs 11:28 reminds us that when we trust in riches we will fall, but the righteous will flourish! Saul could have flourished if he would have chosen to be more concerned with pleasing God than with doing what he wanted to do. David began his life as young man of low degree, but because of his desire to please the Lord, he was exalted to a position of power, and established as the line through which the Messiah would one day come.

WRAP

Choose a verse from today's reading, and follow the steps below.

Write the verse:	Reflect on its meaning:	Apply it to your life:	Pray about today's reading:

Notes & Questions:

Today's Big Idea

The benefits of material wealth will fade away, but the benefits of righteous living are eternal!

Digging Deeper

Psalms David wrote on the Run…

Psalm 57 David trusts the Lord has his refuge

Psalm 59 David seeks rescue from his enemy

Psalm 63 David is thirsting for God's presence

Psalm 142 David seeking hope from God, though the cave felt like prison

If Your Feeling Low in Spirit…

Deuteronomy 31:8 God will never leave you

Isaiah 41:10 God will hold you up and give you strength

Psalm 40: 1-3 God will listen, and he will help you

Matthew 11: 28-30 God will give you rest

Romans 8: 32-38 Nothing can separate you from God's love

God's plan…

Psalm 33:11 stands firm forever

Proverbs 19:21 is not always our plan

Ecclesiastes 3:1 happens at the right time

Romans 8:28 is for our good

Eternal Perspective…

Matthew 5:11-12 gives us hope through persecution

1 Timothy 6:17-19 places our treasure in a firm foundation

Hebrews 12:1-2 Helps us run towards Christ

Day 4

G5278
to stay, to wait; stand ground, bear up against, persevere.

G25 agapaó
love; to love; denotes the love of reason, the love of Christ.

G3985
to make proof of, temptation, test

[12]Blessed is the man that endureth temptation: for
when he is tried, he shall receive the crown of life,
which the Lord hath promised to them that love
him. [13] Let no man say when he is tempted, I am
tempted of God: for God cannot be tempted with
evil, neither tempteth he any man: [14]But every man is
tempted, when he is drawn away of his own lust,
and enticed. [15]Then when lust hath conceived, it
bringeth forth sin: and sin, when it is finished,
bringeth forth death. [16] Do not err, my beloved
brethren.

G1939
Desire, passionate longing

G4815
to collect; to seize, apprehend, conceive, become pregnant.

G2288
death; physical or spiritual

James 1:12-16

Directions: Think of a sin you struggle with and answer the questions below.

1. In what places or situations does this sin become most problematic? Create a plan to navigate these situations.

2. Identify the types of thoughts that precede this sin. What is something you can think on instead during these times.

3. Change the way you view your sin. How can this sin ruin your life or relationships with others?

Daily Devotional

2 Samuel 11-12

The New Testament describes David as a man after God's heart, but David's heart was not always pure before God. There are many recorded sins of King David; his affair with Bathsheba being the most famous. In this story, King David slept with Uriah's wife. After learning that Bathsheba was pregnant, he sent Uriah to the front lines of battle, knowing Uriah would not survive. How did such a God-fearing man wind up in this position?

First, David was not where he was supposed to be. The story begins with David in the palace during the time when men (including kings) go off to war. Had David been in the right place, this sin would not have happened.

Next, while looking out of his window, he saw Bathsheba bathing on her roof top. We might blame Bathsheba for bathing on the roof, but in cultural context this was actually normal. David could have noticed her, and he could have chosen to leave the window and think on other things. He did not.

In life we can't control everything we see. The snares set to pull us from Christ are everywhere, but we can control how we respond. We can remove ourselves from tempting situations. Philippians 4:7-8 says to think on things that are pure, lovely, just, and of good report. We often land in sinful situations when we don't control our thoughts.

Enticed of his own lust, David sent for Bathsheba. From there, their lives grew more complicated as an affair turned into deception, murder, and a shotgun wedding.

In all of this, he did not repent until Nathan, a prophet, approached David with a story of a stolen sheep so that he could finally see his sin through God's eyes. Seeing his sin with the right perspective, led him to repentance. His prayer is recorded in Psalm 51.

We too should be mindful to be in the right place and respond to thoughts in a godly way. If we find ourselves in sin, we need recognize how we got there, repent, and create a plan of action for the future.

Part of repentance is recognizing the destruction sin causes in our lives. We must change the way we view our sin, if we are ever going to seek deliverance from it.

When we repent, God is faithful and just to forgive us our sins. David was not recorded in the New Testament as an adulterer and murderer, but as a man after God's own heart. When we repent, we are covered by the blood of Jesus, we appear before God as His righteous children, and He casts our sin into the sea of forgetfulness.

WRAP

Choose a verse from today's reading, and follow the steps below.

Write the verse:

Reflect on its meaning:

Apply it to your life:

Pray about today's reading:

Notes & Questions:

Today's Big Idea

Temptation is a product of our own desires

Sin can be overcome with the help of Christ!

Digging Deeper

The Sin Problem…

Jeremiah 17:9 The heart is deceitful and wicked

Romans 3:23 We have all sinned

Romans 6:23 The cost of sin is death

The Blood of Christ…

Romans 5:9 Saves us from God's wrath

Ephesians 1:7 Redeems us from sin

Colossians 1:20 Reconciles us to God

1 Peter 1:16-19 Makes us holy

1 John 1:7-10 *cleanses us of all sin*

Overcoming Temptation…

Psalm 119:11 Know the word of God

1 Corinthians 10:13 God will make a way of escape

2 Corinthians 10:5 Line your thoughts up with God's word

Philippians 4:7-8 think on good things

Hebrews 2:18 Christ understands, and He can help us.

We need Repentance…

Proverbs 28:13 we will find mercy

Luke 13:3 It leads to life

Luke 15:7 Heaven rejoices in repentance

Acts 3:19 It wipes out our sins

Day 5

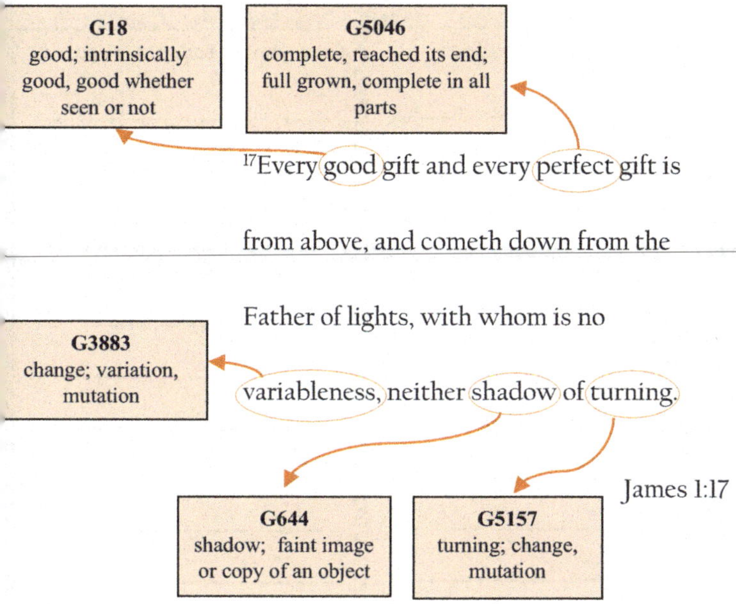

Directions: Think of a difficult season you went through and answer the questions below.

1. How was God faithful to you in the midst of this difficult season?

2. How can God use this season for his glory?

3. What blessings could/have come as a result of this season?

Daily Devotional

Esther 1-10

When things are going badly, we often jump to blaming God for the calamity in our lives, but when things start going well, we forget to thank him. In the midst of great turmoil, Job responded, "the Lord gave, and the Lord hath taken away; blessed be the name of the Lord." [Job 1:21]

Ecclesiastes 3 teaches that there is a season to everything under heaven. There are seasons of sorrow, seasons of joy, and seasons where we just don't know what's happening! In all seasons we can hold on to the promise that God is working behind the scenes and turning all things for the good of those that love him. [Rom. 8:28]

When Esther was taken from her home to the palace, she did not know what her future would hold. If she was not selected as queen, she would become a concubine in the Kings Harem. Being raised to fear the Lord, she may have faced anxious thoughts in the year of preparation before meeting the King. She may have wondered what God was doing, and why these things had happened to her?

While Esther didn't know it in the moment, God had selected her for this specific time and place! He had positioned her perfectly to rescue his people from a disaster that was coming around the corner!

God blessed Esther with favor from the King. After they were married, the King's right-hand man plotted a mass genocide against all of the Jews, her people. This time God used Esther's position and favor with the King to bring to light the wickedness of Haman, his advisor.

A side lesson we can take from this story is that God will not usurp the free will of people. But he will show himself powerful through willing and faithful people that will be courageous and stand with the Lord against wickedness. [2Chron. 16:9]

Just like Job and Esther, we will face challenging seasons in life. When these seasons come, we can stand on the promise that God is an unchanging, good father who gives good gifts. Things will not always make since, but we can trust that God is working in the background for our good.

WRAP

Choose a verse from today's reading, and follow the steps below.

Write the verse:	Reflect on its meaning:	Apply it to your life:	Pray about today's reading:

Notes & Questions:

Today's Big Idea

God is responsible for all the good in our life, and he does not change!

Digging Deeper

God the Good Father…

Matthew 7:11- can do a better job than your earthly father
Matthew 10: 19-20 - guides you in times of trouble
Luke 11:11 - meets the needs of his children
Luke 12:32 - Gladly gives an inheritance
1 John 3:1 - Calls us his children
Hebrews 12:7-11 - disciplines us for our good
  Proverbs 3:12 *- corrects us because he loves us*

The Unchanging God has…

Psalm 136:26 - unchanging love for us
Proverbs 19:21 - unchanging counsel
Isaiah 40:8 -spoken the unchanging word
  Psalm 119:89 *- his word is settled in heaven*
2 Timothy 2:13 -unchanging faithfulness
Hebrews 6:17 - an unchanging purpose

Day 6

[18]Of his own will begat he us with the
word of truth, that we should be a kind of
first fruits of his creatures. [19] Wherefore,
my beloved brethren, let every man be
swift to hear, slow to speak, slow to
wrath: [20]For the wrath of man worketh
not the righteousness of God. [21]
Wherefore lay apart all filthiness and
superfluity of naughtiness and receive
with meekness the engrafted word which
is able to save souls.

James 1: 18-21

G4507
filthy; defilement

G2549
wickedness; evil, vicious disposition, malice spite

G4050
superluity; abundance

G4240
gentleness

G1721
innate, implanted; rooted

Directions: Think of a time you had to deal with difficult personalities and answer the questions below.

1. What opportunities were possibly missed because of your frustration?

2. What character traits could God be trying to develop in you while you work with people you don't get along with?

3. What are some things you can do now, that will help you the next time you're in a situation like this?

Daily Devotional

Numbers 20:1-13

Moses was called to lead God's people from slavery in Egypt to the promise land. Along the journey, Moses and the Israelites faced trials of faith and witnessed the miraculous. They saw the Red Sea parted, were led by a cloud and fire for shade and warmth, they ate manna that fell from heaven, and when they desired meat, God answered them by sending quail! God continuously showed devotion, faithfulness and love to his children. With all that they witnessed, the Israelites would still doubt God, disobey Him, create false idols, and constantly complain. Leading this group was filled with frustration for sure!

One day, when the people were in need of water, God instructed Moses to go and strike a rock. He obeyed, and water flowed from it to nourish all of Israel and their livestock. A little while later, they needed water again. This time, God instructed Moses to speak to the rock, and that water would flow from it. Frustrated with all the people's grumbling, Moses walked up to the rock and struck it twice, saying "Listen you rebels, must we bring you water out of this rock?" and the water came forth, just like before.

In his anger, Moses made two errors. In anger, he struck the rock twice instead of speaking to it. Then, He tried to take God's place by doing what he thought best. He did not trust God, so he disobeyed Him.

In 1 Corinthians 10 we learn that God was using the rock as a representation of Christ. Christ took our punishment on the cross. From that point on, life giving water has flowed for all! Now, when we're running on empty, and need more spiritual water from the Lord, we don't have to go punish Christ again, to get that water. We can just speak to the Lord and the life-giving water flows to nourish our soul.

God wanted to use Moses to teach this important lesson to his people, and to display a shadow of things to come. Unfortunately, the wrath of Moses resulted in a missed opportunity.

Christ has called us to be his ambassadors, so we are often presented with opportunities to show the goodness of God to others. Like Moses, we can become frustrated when dealing with other people. We lose sight of the fact that we are all created by God, and that he has a plan for each of us.

Because of this, it is so important that we take to heart the lesson from James in today's reading. We need to be intentional about laying aside those things that do not portray the character of God in our lives. When tempers flare it's easy to lose sight of what God is trying to accomplish in a situation.

That is why it is so important that we humble ourselves and receive God's word into our lives. His word is able to change our hearts to be more like His. The more we become like the Lord, the easier it is to put our sinful nature behind us, and stay in tune with what God desires to accomplish in each situation of our lives.

WRAP

Choose a verse from today's reading, and follow the steps below.

Write the verse:

Reflect on its meaning:

Apply it to your life:

Pray about today's reading:

Notes & Questions:

Today's Big Idea

Focusing on our frustration can cause us to miss what God wants to do in a situation

Digging Deeper

When your stressed, trust that…

Psalm 46:10 God is bigger than the problem
Psalm 55:22 God will sustain you
Psalm 121:1-2 God will help you
Jeremiah 29:11 God has a plan for you
Colossians 3:15 God has peace for you in this moment

All people are created by God…

Genesis 1:27 in His own image.
Romans 1:6 to have a relationship with Him
Ephesians 2:10 for good works through Christ
2 Timothy 1:9 and called to a holy calling
1 Timothy 2:3-4 *God's will is that all would be saved*
Matthew 22:14 *We have to answer the call*

Obedience…

Deuteronomy 5:33 leads to a long life
Psalm 68:5-6 leads to God's provision in your life
John 7:17 helps you to identify false teaching
John 15:10 causes you to abide in the love of Christ

Day 7

Special Note
eth endings – defined as an archaic suffix,

When a verb ends in an eth it represents the present tense - this is happening **right now**!

While it's debated, many view this tense to indicate a continuous state of the verb.

Ex: goeth – they are going right now, **or** they are continuously going.

G3884
to mislead

G2707
mirror

22 But be ye doers of the word, and not hearers
only, deceiving your own selves. 23 For if any be
a hearer of the word, and not a doer, he is like
unto a man beholding his natural face in a glass:
24 For he beholdeth himself, and goeth his way,
and straightway forgetteth what manner of
man he was. 25 But whoso looketh into the
perfect law of liberty, and continueth therein,
he being not a forgetful hearer, but a doer of the
work, this man shall be blessed in his deed.

James 1:22-25

Romans 8:2
In Christ, we are set free from the law of sin and death.

Directions: Answer the questions below

1. What is something God has recently spoken to you about through his word?

2. Brainstorm a couple of ways you can become a doer with what God has been showing you.

3. Create a plan you can put into action within the next 24 hours.

Daily Devotional

1 Kings 11-13

Due to Solomon's disobedience, God promised to tear apart the kingdom of Israel during the reign of his son. Before Solomon died, a prophet came to tell Jeroboam that God was about to tear apart the kingdom of Israel. For the sake of David and Jerusalem, God would preserve two tribes for David's lineage. As for the other ten tribes, God would give them to Jeroboam. God promised Jeroboam that if he remained faithful as David had, then He would establish Jeroboam just like He had established David.

After Solomon's death, God kept his promise, and Jeroboam became the ruler over the ten northern tribes of Israel. Unfortunately, Jeroboam did not trust the word of the Lord. He became fearful of what would happen when the Israelites traveled to Jerusalem to make their sacrifices to God. So he built two golden calves and instructed the people of Israel to not go down to Jerusalem, and to instead bring their sacrifices to these false idols and worship God there.

This angered the Lord, so he sent a man of God to confront Jeroboam. At the word of this Man, Jeroboam's hand was shriveled, the altar was torn down, and ash came from the altar. Upon Jeroboam's request, the man sought for the Lord to restore Jeroboam's hand, and God did. Knowing that this man was truly a prophet from the Lord, Jeroboam invited the man to stay for dinner. However, the man said no. God had clearly instructed him to not stop for dinner with anyone and to go home a different way than he came.

While on his way, A false prophet stopped him, and lied to him, saying that an Angel had come to him with a message from God to bring the young man home and to feed him. The young Man of God believed the lies of the false prophet, and went to his home for a meal. But, while he was there, the Lord gave a true word to the old prophet, and he told the young man that the consequence for his disobedience would be death.

Sure enough, the following day, the young man of God fell from his donkey and was killed by a lion on his way home. The lion and the donkey stood by the man and he was not eaten. The old prophet came and found him, and buried him.

The Lord spoke to Jeroboam and told him to remain faithful. At the first fear, Jeroboam disobeyed God. He heard the word, but he did not obey the word. Likewise, the young man of God heard the word the Lord. Initially he acted on it, and through him, God displayed his power to the king. But on his way home a deceiver tricked him into believing that the word he had heard was false.

So many times, we hear a word from the Lord, and then we walk away and do not act on what the Lord has spoken to us. A word from the Lord will most commonly come from our time reading the Bible, a convicting or challenging sermon, or even an insight to scripture from a brother or sister in Christ. When these situations arise, God is trying to get our attention and be the guide to our path.

Like Jeroboam and the man of God, we deceive ourselves into believing that we know best, and we stop acting on God's clear instructions that he has given us in His word.

Unlike these two men, let's make the decision to be intentional about looking into the law of liberty that we have obtained through Christ Jesus, and continuing to heed the word of the Lord. Let's make the decision today to not be a forgetful hearer, but to also be a doer of God's word!

WRAP

Choose a verse from today's reading, and follow the steps below.

Write the verse:	Reflect on its meaning:	Apply it to your life:	Pray about the reading:

Notes & Questions:

Today's Big Idea

*Be a doer of God's word

*If God is showing you something to do in His word, be faithful to do it!

Digging Deeper

Doers of God's Word…

Matthew 7:24 are wise, and build on the rock

Luke 11:28 are blessed

Romans 2:13 will be justified

We are saved by faith, not works, but faith produces works.

Forgetful hearers…

Luke 6:46-49 build without a foundation

2 Timothy 3:6-7 are led astray by passions

Luke 14:12-15 struggle to believe, obey, and love Christ

The Law…

Psalms 19:7-9 is perfect, converts the soul, and opens eyes

Romans 7:7 teaches us what sin is

1 Timothy 1:8-10 was made for the lawless

The New Covenant…

Jeremiah 31:33 has written the law on our hearts

Galatians 5:13-18 provides liberty to serve one another in love

Hebrews 9:15 redeems us from the transgressions of the law

Day 8

G2357
religious; devout

G2513
clean; guiltless, upright

G5468
to lead with a bridle; restrain

G3152
useless

G784
spotless, undefiled, pure

26 If any man among you seems religious and
bridleth not his tongue, but deceiveth his
own heart, this man's religion is vain. 27 Pure
religion and undefiled before God and the
Father is this, to visit the fatherless and
widows in their affliction, and to keep
himself unspotted from the world.

James 1:26-27

Directions: Work through the challenges below.

1. As you go throughout your day ask God to help you notice the needs of others. Write down any needs that stand out to you.

2. Ask God for ideas and wisdom to meet some of the needs you noticed.

3. Choose one these ideas to put into action!

Daily Devotional

Luke 10:25-37

In the parable of the Good Samaritan, a man is robbed and left for dead. The first two people to pass him by were seemingly religious men, a priest and a Levite. These religious men would have been able to quote scripture, say eloquent prayers, and talk theology at great length. However, when the rubber met the road, and the time came to walk out their religious principles, they chose to do nothing. They saw the dying man, and they passed by him on the other side of the road.

The third person to come along was a Samaritan. Without hesitation, the Samaritan took care of his neighbor. Interestingly, Samaritans are a people group that were despised by most Jews during this time. The Samaritan knew he couldn't meet all the man's needs on his own, so he took the man to the inn keeper who could. Then he gave of his own resources to ensure the cost of the man's needs were covered, while the inn keeper saw to his care.

In this parable we're reminded that it doesn't matter how religious you look on the outside if you're not willing to live out your faith when God presents you with the opportunities to do so.

Christianity is not a spectator sport. Participation is essential to fulfill the will of the Father during our time on earth. 2 Chronicles 16:9 tells us that God's eyes search the earth to show himself powerful on behalf of those who have the right heart towards Him. God's will is accomplished when we submit to him as willing and yielded vessels, continuing the work Christ began.

Imagine for a moment that the Samaritan didn't stop. What would have become of the man who was robbed? Imagine your life, if no one ever shared the good news of Jesus Christ with you. Where would you be?

Yesterday we learned that God wants us to not be hearers of the word only, but doers also. Today We focus on not just growing in the Lord for ourselves, but using what we've learned in our growth to participate as a co-laborer with Christ in leading others to life changing salvation.

True religion is not talking a good game. True religion is walking out your faith with love and compassion for those that are beat, bruised, and left for dead by sin; to pick them up and get them to the inn keeper who can continue seeing after their care, and to give of our own resources when needed to meet the physical needs while God tends to the spiritual ones.

WRAP

Choose a verse from today's reading, and follow the steps below.

Write the verse:

Reflect on its meaning:

Apply it to your life:

Pray about today's reading:

Notes & Questions:

Today's Big Idea

Following Jesus isn't about the talk. It's all about the walk!

Digging Deeper

Vain Religion...

Matthew 16:1-4 will have you seeking signs more than Christ

Matthew 23:13-15 can harm others as they seek Christ

Matthew 23:25-28 looks pretty on the outside, but ignores the inside

Matthew 23:29-33 will cause you to miss the will of God

Christian Conduct & Speech...

Galatians 5:25 is led by the Holy Spirit

Ephesians 5:15-21 does the will of the Lord

Colossians 4:5-6 shows wisdom, grace, and be seasoned with salt (i.e., bringing out the best in others)

1 Peter 1:14-16 shall be holy

True Religion...

Micah 6:8 does justice, loves mercy, & walks humbly with God.

John 17:1-3 starts with accepting eternal life through Christ to know the one true God.

Romans 13:10 shows love to neighbors

Day 9

G2129
hold

G4382
respect of persons; partiality, favoritism

[1] My brethren, have not the faith of our Lord Jesus
Christ, the Lord of glory, with respect of persons. [2]
For if there come unto your assembly a man with a
gold ring, in goodly apparel, and there come in also
a poor man in vile raiment; [3] And ye have respect to
him that weareth the gay clothing, and say unto
him, sit thou here in a good place; and say to the
poor, stand thou there, or sit here under my
footstool: [4] Are ye not then partial in yourselves,
and are become judges of evil thoughts?

G2986
Bright; shining, magnificent, splendid

G1252 to distinguish; separate

James 2:1-5

Directions: Answer the questions below.

1. Describe a time when you showed preference for or against someone. What was your motivation for doing this?

2. How was this preference harmful to the body of Christ?

Daily Devotional

Luke 19:1-10

Over the next few days, the text from James deals with the treatment of the poor and favoritism towards the rich. At the time of this writing, many middle-class Christians were showing special preference to the rich for personal gain, and the rich were taking advantage of the poor. Those of better means were becoming prideful and high minded. Rather than having love for the poor, they thought themselves better than them. Their focus was on the temporal gain that could be made on earth, rather than the eternal gains awaiting them in heaven. This behavior is harmful to the body of Christ.

Regarding doctrine, it seems that the pendulum swings from one extreme to the next. Often the extremes are formed as reactions to the flaws in the last popular teaching, rather than being formed as a balanced approach to what is actually stated in the Bible.

Teaching on money is no different. Some will act as though its criminal for a preacher to drive anything nicer than a rusted jalopy, or have a food budget that affords more than ramen. Others will buy into a prosperity gospel, thinking that faith is the currency you pop into God's vending machine and anything you desire will be manifested within the fortnight. While scripture can be twisted to fit either narrative, that does not make it God's blueprint for our lives.

Rather than finding a story that closely aligns to today's text, we will look at Zacchaeus as a model for how an encounter with Christ should change the way we look at money.

Zacchaeus, a chief tax collector, was so desperate to see Jesus he climbed up in a sycamore tree. As Jesus passed by, he called to Zacchaeus to inform him that he'd be visiting his home! In his encounter with Christ, Zacchaeus declared that he would give half his wealth to the poor, and repay all the people he'd cheated on their taxes four times over.

Before Christ, Zacchaeus was corrupt and full of greed. After encountering Christ, he decided to make retribution for his past corruption, and lead a generous life.

Jesus reminds us in the gospel of Luke that where our treasure is, our heart will be also. God does not demand us to be poor, but he does expect us to love him more than our wealth. He expected Zacchaeus to repay what he'd stolen, and to conduct fair business in the future. He expects us not to take advantage of the misfortune of others, and to treat the poor with the same dignity of all other people.

To those that tried to curry favor with the rich for personal gain, James instructs them that this is against the law of God. Showing favoritism is not loving your neighbor as yourself. The question becomes: are we trusting God for our provision? Or are we trusting the rich? Paul wrote to the Philippians that he knew both how to be abased and how to abound, and in both he learned to be content. To the Colossians, he said to do all our work with all our heart, as though we were doing it unto the Lord. As followers of Christ, we should do our best in our line of work, be wise stewards of the resources we've been blessed with, and give generously as the Lord leads our hearts.

Ultimately, we should see our wealth from the standpoint that it has been entrusted into our stewardship by the Lord, to whom it still belongs, as provision for our household and to fulfill his purposes. Our hearts should be more concerned with the development of our brethren, than our bank balance.

WRAP

Choose a verse from today's reading, and follow the steps below.

Write the verse:	Reflect on its meaning:	Apply it to your life:	Pray about today's reading:

Notes & Questions:

Today's Big Idea

God is not a respecter of persons, and we shouldn't be either!

Digging Deeper

If you are Prideful or high minded…

Proverbs 13:10 there will be contention around you

Proverbs 29:23 God will bring you low

Pr. 11:2, Pr. 16:8, Pr. 18:12, Is. 2:12

Jeremiah 9:23-24 you can bring yourself low by glorying in God rather than yourself

2 Cor. 10:17-18, Ro. 11:18-20, Ga 6:14

Takeaway: Pride causes problems, and God does not like it. You can deal with your pride, or God will deal with your pride. Things will run much smoother if you deal with it.

Things of Earth...

1Peter 1:24 do not last

Ps 49:12, Ps 103: 15-16, Isaiah 40:6-7

Eternal Thinking...

2 Corinthians 4:17-5:7 keeps our faith strong in hard times

Luke 21:33 reminds us that his word is true and unchanging

Colossians 4:2-6 keeps us on mission, redeeming the time

Day 10

G2818
heir, those who become children of God and inherit the privileges of the Messianic Kingdom through Christ.

G4434
one who crouches or cowers; a beggar.

G818
dishonored

G2616
Exercise power over; accuse

G987
to speak lightly or profanely of sacred things

5 Hearken, my beloved brethren, Hath not
God chosen the poor of this world rich in
faith, and heirs of the kingdom which he
hath promised to them that love him? 6 But
ye have despised the poor. Do not rich men
oppress you, and draw you before the
judgment seats? 7 Do not they blaspheme
that worthy name by the which ye are
called?

James 2:5-7

Directions: Respond to the prompts below, and describe the lessons that can be taken from each life experience.

1. Describe a time when you wanted something you could not have. How did you respond?

2. Describe a time you cared more about people's thoughts of you than God's thoughts of you.

Daily Devotional

1 Kings 21

Near King Ahab's palace, lived a man named Naboth. Naboth owned a vineyard that had been in his family for many generations. Due to the vineyard's proximity to the palace, Ahab wanted to buy it and turn it into a vegetable garden, so he offered Naboth his choice of money or a better vineyard. Because the vineyard had been the inheritance of Naboth's ancestors, he had no interest in the King's offer.

Ahab did not take this rejection well. Ahab's wife Jezebel assured him that he didn't need to worry; she would get him the vineyard he desired. Jezebel's plan involved bringing Naboth in front of the court and then having two men wrongly testify that he had cursed God and the King. When the plan had come to fruition, Naboth was stoned to death.

After hearing of his death, Ahab went down to claim the vineyard for his vegetable garden. However, he was met by Elijah the prophet who had been sent to him with a message from the Lord. Elijah questioned Ahab on both killing Naboth and then coming to take possession of his land. Then, he went on to tell Ahab that because he sold himself to wickedness in the sight of the Lord, that God would respond by cutting Ahab off from all the men of Israel, destroy his royal house, and that the dogs would lick up his blood in the place that Naboth died.

Sadly, this sort of corruption is still present in our world today among those with great wealth and power, and it does not go unnoticed by God. James references that those with wealth and power were oppressing the poor in the church. Even worse the average Joes of the church were siding with the wealthy and despising the poor too. They wanted to get the favor of the wealthy. The saddest part for the panderers, is that to the wicked and corrupt everyone is merely a disposable means to an end.

It's interesting that one of the things Naboth was charged with was cursing God, when Jezebel herself worshipped Baal. Jezebel did not care one bit for the God of Israel. Neither did the corrupt in the days of James, nor do the corrupt in our world today. None the less, they will surely bring accusations against believers for their lack of devotion to Christ and his teachings.

In today's church we often look down on the poor for no reason at all. We cast judgement, do not offer help, and often exclude the "less desirables" from association. Jesus himself said that the poor will be with you always. He had compassion for the poor, and routinely shunned the rich. Not because money is bad, but because of what the love of money did to many that Jesus came in contact with.

We must be vigilant each day to treat people with equal dignity and respect, not giving preference to others based on their station in life. Let's make a point to align ourself with those things that are good and right in God's sight, and to not align ourselves with the trending wickedness of the day. When we side with wickedness, whether for favor, comfort, or any other reason, we are no better than the two false witnesses. In their cooperation with Jezebel, they condemned an innocent man to death. When we cooperate with evil, we are in danger of doing the same thing.

WRAP

Choose a verse from today's reading, and follow the steps below.

Write the verse:

Reflect on its meaning:

Apply it to your life:

Pray about today's reading:

Notes & Questions:

Today's Big Idea

Do what is right in God's eyes, rather than siding with what is favorable among people.

Digging Deeper

Care for the poor…

Leviticus 19:15 we are commanded to be just and impartial regarding the poor

Deuteronomy 15:7-11 We should not harden our heart or shut our hands to the poor. There will always be those that are poor.

Psalm 41:1-3 Blessings come to those that care for the poor

Proverbs 19:17 God repays those that help the poor.

Isaiah 58:10 it makes you feel better

Luke 14:13 include the poor in activities

Those Exploiting & Neglecting the Poor…

Proverbs 17:5 insult God, and will not go unpunished.

Proverbs 22:16 & 22-23

Proverbs 21:13 will not be answered when calling out to God.

1 John 3:17 show a lack of God's love within them

People Pleasing…

Proverbs 29:25 is a trap

Psalm 118:8 - God is a better refuge than people

John 12:42-43 makes serving God harder

Galatians 1:10

Acts 5:27-32 a story of Peter refusing to be a people pleaser

Day 11

G937
belonging to the king; preeminent; surpassing all others

G1651
to expose, convict or reprove; to show as guilty

G25 agapaó
love; to love; denotes the love of reason, the love of Christ.

G3848
one who stands beside; a law-breaker

8 If ye fulfil the royal law according to
scripture, Thou shalt love thy neighbor as
thyself, ye do well: 9 But if ye have respecter
of persons, ye commit sin, and are convinced
of the law as transgressors. 10 For whosoever
shall keep the whole law, and yet offend in
one point, he is guilty of all.

James 2:8-10

Directions: Answer each of the questions below.

1. How would you feel knowing that you could do everything right, and one mistake would bring the wrath of God your way?

2. How would your life be different living under the law? Would you try harder to do well or give up under the hopelessness of it? Explain.

3. How does this knowledge change your perspective of the gift we have in Christ?

Daily Devotional

2 Chronicles 18-19 & 1 Kings 22

King Jehoshaphat reigned in the ways of the Lord. He removed the places of idol worship throughout Judah, did away with cult prostitution, and he sent priests to every town to teach the people God's laws.

As a result, the fear of the Lord fell on the surrounding nations, so that none of them attacked Judah. During this time, Judah experienced an economic boom, more fortresses were built, storage cities were created, and the military increased in number and might.

However, Jehoshaphat's weakness was that he viewed the Kingdom of Israel as a friend. They had the same ancestry, and were both called to be the people of God. But the leadership of Israel was continuously wicked. Throughout his reign, he entered into three unholy alliances with Israel, which cost the kingdom greatly.

First, he married his son Jehoram to Athaliah, the daughter of Ahab and Jezebel. Athaliah would wreak havoc on Judah for years to come. She would turn her husband and sons to the worship of Baal, usurp the throne of Judah, and attempt to kill every male in the lineage of David. Only Joash would escape and come back to reign.

The second was agreeing to a military alliance with Ahab against the Syrians. Jehoshaphat placed the condition on Ahab that he would only agree after hearing from the prophets. All of Ahab's prophets spoke favorably of the war. Recognizing that these prophets did not speak for God, Jehoshaphat called for a prophet of the Lord. Micaiah came and said that God showed him that this battle would be used by God for the death of Ahab.

Even though he knew his ally was promised death, Jehoshaphat marched his men right into battle. He even let Ahab talk him into wearing his royal robes, while King Ahab dressed as a common soldier so that the enemies would mistake Jehoshaphat for Ahab. Thankfully, the Lord delivered Jehoshaphat. Despite the ploy, Ahab was killed by a stray arrow.

When Jehoshaphat returned home, the prophet Jehu confronted him for helping those who are wicked and loving those who hate the Lord. Jehu told him God's judgement was against him, but he was spared because there was some good in him. [2 Chron. 19: 1-3] Jehoshaphat got back to doing the work of the Lord, and reaped the rewards of God's blessings on his people, until he entered into a trade alliance with new king of Israel to build ships. God caused the ships to wreck because of the alliance, he later died, and his son became King.

Jehoshaphat lived his whole life honoring God's law, but one area of transgression caused his reign to be cut short, and led to many years of turmoil for Judah at the hands of Athaliah.

Galatians 3:23-24 states that the law was given as a tutor, teaching concepts that bring us to Christ. Paul wrote in Romans that he would not even know he had committed sin, if the law wasn't there to reveal what sin was. When we try to live by the letter of the law, we have to understand that transgressing in one area is the same as transgressing all of it. Like Jehoshaphat, none of us can keep every part of the law faithfully. The consequence for these transgressions is the same. Thankfully we now live under a better covenant where we can come to God with a repentant heart and receive mercy rather than justice when we fall short.

WRAP

Choose a verse from today's reading, and follow the steps below.

Write the verse:	Reflect on its meaning:	Apply it to your life:	Pray about today's reading:

Notes & Questions:

Today's Big Idea

*Living under the law is hard!

*Transgressing the law in one area, makes the transgressor guilty of the whole law.

Digging Deeper

The law is useful…

Psalm 119:165 those that follow it have grace, peace, and do not stumble

Matthew 5:27-28 It shows us the condition of man

Romans 7:12 - It reflects God's character

Galatians 3:21-24 It is a tutor

The law in the New Covenant…

Romans 3:19-20 It cannot save us

Galatians 3:10-14 those that live under it are under a curse

Galatians 4:21-31 human effort to keep it, lashes out against grace

Grace by the Blood of Christ…

John 3:16 was given because God loves us

Matthew 5:18 does not cancel the law, but fulfills it

all the ceremonial pieces were fulfilled in Christ, the moral law of God is still very much in affect, and we would be wise to obey it to the best of our ability.

Romans 2:14-15 writes the law on our hearts, and we do it by nature

Day 12

11 For he that said, do not commit adultery,
said also, Do not kill. Now if thou commit
no adultery, yet if thou kill, thou art become
a transgressor of the law. 12 So speak ye, and
so do, as they that shall be judged by the law
of liberty. 13 For he shall have judgment
without mercy, that hath shewed no mercy;
and mercy rejoiceth against judgment.

G2620
To exult over; triumph over, boast against

James 2:11-13

Directions: Answer the questions below.

1. Describe a time you confronted someone with their sin. What did you get right? What do you wish you had done better?

2. Describe a time that you withheld forgiveness from someone because they didn't deserve it. How did you come to a place of forgiveness for them? If you haven't forgiven them yet, why should you?

Daily Devotional

John 8:3-11 & Matthew 18:21-35

John 8 opens with Jesus teaching at the temple, when the scribes and pharisees bring before him an adulteress woman – caught in the very act! They remind Jesus that the Levitical Law, says that an adulteress should be stoned, and inquire of Jesus what he has to say about it. It should be noted that the Law required stoning for both the man and woman committing adultery.

Initially, Jesus stooped down, wrote in the dirt, and pretended not to hear them. When they continued, he stood up and said "He that is without sin among you, let him cast a stone at her." [John 8:7] The Pharisees and Scribes were convicted by their own conscience and walked away, leaving the woman standing there.

Jesus asked her, "Woman, where are those thine accusers? Hath no man condemned thee?' She said, 'No man, Lord.' And Jesus said, 'Neither do I condemn thee; go, and sin no more.'" [John 8:10-11]

Those that have heard this story, have heard it said that Jesus was the only one without sin, with a clear conscience, still standing there, able to throw a stone, and he chose not to. Rather than condemning her to death, he gave her the instruction to "go, and sin no more." The gift of Christ is that he offers a call to repentance, where the law laid condemnation. Where sin requires justice, his blood, shed on the cross, provides mercy.

Yesterday, we focused on the judgment that comes when we transgress the law. We shouldn't trash the law. It is still a tutor that teaches right from wrong. The royal law of God is preeminent. It surpasses all other laws of man. There is no equal to it. When we line ourselves up against it, we are made to see our need for a Savior!

Glory be to God that he has sent that Savior, Jesus Christ! Today we reap the rewards of the law of liberty! Romans 8:2 says that in Christ, we are set free from the law of sin and death. That means that when we have accepted Christ as the sacrifice for our sin, and chosen to die to ourselves, and live for Him, we get the blessing of mercy substituted in our lives where the law would have required a just judgement.

Like Christ, we should also show mercy to others. In the parable of the unmerciful servant. A man's large debt is completely cancelled. No sooner than his debt is cancelled, he goes after a man who owed him a small amount, and ruthlessly throws the man into prison when he can't pay. When the King heard what had happened, he came after the man whose debt he cancelled. He threw the wicked servant to jailers to be tortured.

As Christians, we sometimes forget that Christ has forgiven such a large debt in us. We want mercy for ourselves, but when it comes to others, we rush to judgment. We can be cruel and harsh and harm their pursuit of the Lord. This is not to say we should excuse sin. Christ himself said "go, and sin no more". Rather, in love we should point others to repentance and the mercy that is provided by the shed blood of Christ at Calvary.

WRAP

Choose a verse from today's reading, and follow the steps below.

Write the verse:

Reflect on its meaning:

Apply it to your life:

Pray about today's reading:

Notes & Questions:

Today's Big Idea

Show mercy as you have been shown mercy.

Digging Deeper

Righteous Judgments…

Zechariah 8:16 are based on truth and lead to peace
Matthew 7:6 are given with discernment
John 7:24 are not based on appearances
Galatians 6:1 should work to restore one's relationship with Christ
Ephesians 5:11 expose evil

Warnings about Judgement…

Ezekiel 3:18-19 you will be held accountable for your silence.
Matthew 7:1-2 you will be judged by the same standard you judge others
Matthew 7:3-5 fix yourself before trying to fix others
Romans 2:1-2 & 21-22 practice what you preach

Mercy for ourselves and others…

Matthew 5:7 the merciful will receive mercy
Luke 6:36 show mercy, God has been merciful
Ephesians 2:4 God is rich in mercy because he loves us
Hebrews 4:16 God's grace and mercy is there when we need it

Day 13

G80
a brother; member of the same religious community

G3007
leave behind; wanting, fall short of

G5526
to feed, fatten, fill, satisfy

G3498
dead; lifeless, a corpse

14 What doth it profit, my brethren, though a man
say he hath faith, and have not works? Can faith
save him? 15 If a brother or sister be naked, and
destitute of daily food, 16 And one of you say unto
them, depart in peace, be ye warmed and filled;
notwithstanding ye give them not those things
which are needful to the body; what doth it profit?
17 Even so faith, if it hath not works is dead, being
alone. 18 Yea, a man may say, Thou hast faith, and I
have works: shew me thy faith without thy works,
and I will shew thee my faith by my works.

James 2:14-18

Directions: Respond to the prompts below.

1. What step of faith do you feel the Lord is calling you take right now?

2. What obstacles are in your way from taking that step of faith?

3. Create a plan of action to take a step of faith this week.

Daily Devotional

Matthew 25:31-46

When teaching on the coming judgement, Jesus tells everyone that the righteous and unrighteous will be separated. He will commend the righteous for how they cared for him. When they ask, "when did we do all these things for you?" he will answer, "Truly I tell you, whatever you did for one of the least of these brothers and sisters of mine, you did for me." [Matt. 25:40]

The unrighteous on the other hand, will ask "Lord, when did we see you hungry or thirsty or a stranger or needing clothes or sick or in prison, and did not help you?" [Matt. 25:44] The answer will similarly be, when you didn't help others, you didn't help me.

Today, faith is often treated like a spiritual debit card that you stick in God's vending machine, and watch all your dreams pop out. What a shame to make such a mockery of the precious substance that faith is in the heart of a believer. How disheartening it is for those seeking to apply faith in their lives, when the magic vending machine doesn't fulfill their wishes. We often ridicule them for a lack of faith. What a disgrace. Faith is not a magic debit card. Faith at its core is expressed by love in action.

What emboldened the Hebrew children, facing the furnace, to say to Nebuchadnezzar "But if not, be it known unto thee, O king, that we will not serve thy gods, nor worship the golden image which thou hast set up." [Dan.3:18]? It was a deep love for God that spurred them to action.

After being jailed, tortured, and even martyred, what caused the Christians of Acts to rise up, saying we will not stop preaching the name of Jesus? It was love of God and a love for the lost that motivated them to act.

A relationship with God will lead you to love him. The more you love him, the more your heart will mirror his. You will see this world through his perspective. You won't look at sin the same, you won't look at your life the same, and you won't look at the people the same ever again.

This change in you, will stir your heart, and it will motivate you to do something. It'll be scary at first. There will be discouraging obstacles holding you back, but as you continuously turn love into action, faith will grow. It will strengthen under the stress of this world as a muscle strengthens under the stress of weight. As you exercise your growing faith, you will find God faithful. You will see his goodness in places you used to only see despair. You will build an arsenal of knowledge based on the goodness of God in your life. You will stand on that knowledge troubling times. Your faith will be strong, and you will be bold!

Works did not bring us into the family of Christ, but in the family of Christ, we have work to do. Jesus gave us a new command to love one another, as he has loved us. By that love, everyone would know that we are his disciples [John 13:34-35]. Part of following Christ, is learning to look at others through his perspective, and loving them as he would! This kind of love, is not just lip service! This kind of love produces action. It is the outward expression of our faith.

WRAP

Choose a verse from today's reading, and follow the steps below.

Write the verse:	Reflect on its meaning:	Apply it to your life:	Pray about today's reading:

Notes & Questions:

Today's Big Idea

Works didn't make us part of God's family.

As part of God's family, we have work to do!

Digging Deeper

One is who is Justified is…

Romans 4:6-8 forgiven of all sin
Romans 5:1 at peace with God
Titus 3:5-7 an heir of God
__Romans 8:17__ heirs of God, and co-heirs with Christ. We will suffer with him, and also be glorified with him.

Carnal Believers…

Romans 8:6 focus on their flesh - causing spiritual death
Romans 8:7 are hostile towards God, and do not submit to him.
Galatians 5:17 are at war within themselves
1 Corinthians 3:1-3 do not experience spiritual growth

Caring for others…

Matthew 25:31-46 is caring for Christ
John 13:34-35 shows that we are followers of Christ
James 1:27 is true religion
1 John3:17-18 reveals that God's love is in you

Day 14

G4100 to have faith.

G1344 to deem right.

G2756 empty, fruitless

G4903 To work together

G2041 Work, task, employment

G5048 Bring to an end, finish, accomplish, fulfill

19 Thou believest that there is one God; thou doest
well: the devils also believe and tremble. 20 But wilt
thou know, O vain man, that faith without works is
dead? 21 Was not Abraham our father justified by
works, when he had offered Isaac his son upon the
altar? 22 Seest thou how faith wrought with his
works, and by works was faith made perfect? 23 And
the scripture was fulfilled which saith, Abraham
believed God and it was imputed unto him for
righteousness: and he was called the Friend of God.

G3049 to reckon, consider; count, charge with, conclude, think, suppose

James 2:19-23

Directions: Respond to the prompts below with a situation past or present.

1. Describe a sacrificial step of faith that God has placed on your heart to do.

2. What concerns or obstacles are holding you back from acting?

3. What promises from God's word can you hold onto to help you make this step of faith?
Do a little digging if needed!

Daily Devotional

Genesis 22:1-19 & Hebrews 11:17-19

At the age of 75, Abraham was called to leave his home and follow God with the promise that God was going to make a great nation through his line. Abraham believed God and obeyed, even though he and his wife, Sarah, age 65, were childless. Abraham faithfully followed God for 25 years before the promised son was born.

Years later, God tested Abraham by asking that he sacrifice his son. To the modern mind, this seems so cruel and unexpected, especially when considering that this promised son, was supposed to be the heir that God would use to create a great nation. Scholars often point out that during this time in history child sacrifice was normal across Mesopotamia and Canaan, and would not have seemed to be an unusual request. The sacrifice of one's own child would show significant devotion to the gods.

However, Hebrews 11:17-19 gives a better glimpse into the mind of Abraham. Abraham took God at his word, and knew that God did not lie. God had promised Abraham that his descendants would come through Isaac. So, rather than chalking up God's request to a test of mere devotion, he recognized that some greater purpose would be achieved through this act. In verse 19 it says that Abraham believed God would raise Isaac back up from the dead. When leaving for his journey, Genesis records that Abraham said he and the boy would return [Gen. 22:5].

Once they arrived in Moriah, Abraham prepared the altar to sacrifice Isaac to the Lord, fully placing his trust in God that he would be faithful to His word. Before Abraham took the life of his son, an angel of the Lord appeared and stopped the process. Abraham had shown himself faithful to God, and God had provided a ram in the thicket.

In addition to proving the faith of Abraham, this story serves as a foreshadowing of Christ. While other gods required the sacrifice of children as a show of devotion or to obtain favor, our God does not. Instead, he sacrificed his son as a show of his devotion to us, so that we can be reconciled to him and obtain his favor. Abraham believed that God would raise his son from the dead. God prepared a ram in the thicket to be the sacrifice. Christ is the lamb that stood in the place and became the sacrifice for us, and he was raised to life again.

Yesterday, I described faith as love in action. Abraham's love of God pushed him into obedient action. With his step of faith, God showed himself faithful. God has magnified his word above his name [Psalm 138:2] and he cannot lie [Titus 1:2]. He is worthy of our trust and devotion in all situations.

WRAP

Choose a verse from today's reading, and follow the steps below.

Write the verse:

Reflect on its meaning:

Apply it to your life:

Pray about today's reading:

Notes & Questions:

Digging Deeper

The Demons believe there is one God…

Matthew 8:29 they recognized Jesus as the Son of God, and wanted to know why he'd come to punish them before the appointed time

Mark 1:23-24, Mark 3:11, Mark 3:22-27, Mark 5:7

Matthew 10:12 Jesus gave his disciples authority over unclean spirits.

Luke 10:17

Acts 19:13-16 Seven Sons of Sceva were beat up after trying to cast out demons; the demons knew Jesus and Paul, but not them.

Faith produces work…

Galatians 5:6 works of the law don't produce anything of value, faith that works by love is what matters

Ephesians 2:8-10 we were created to do good works

1 Thessalonians 1:3 work is produced by faith and prompted by love

Faith grows…

Romans 4: 20-21 by believing God's word

Romans 10:17 by reading God's word

James 1:22-24 by doing God's word

Today's Big Idea

Look at trials as an opportunity for development!

Day 15

24 Ye see then how that by works a man is
justified, and not by faith only. 25 Likewise
also was not Rahab the harlot justified by
works, when she had received the
messengers, and had sent them out another
way? 26 For as the body without the spirit is
dead, so faith without works is dead also.

G3498
dead; lifeless, subject to death, a corpse

James 2:24-26

Directions: Use this space to share your testimony of how you came to follow Christ.

Daily Devotional

Joshua 2 & 6

After entering the promise land, Joshua sent to spies ahead to scout Jericho, a well-fortified city. The inhabitants of Jericho had heard of all the miracles and victories that God had accomplished for his people during their years in the wilderness. Rehab recognized that the God they served was the living God. She was so certain of this fact, that she hid the spies from her king. In doing this she became a traitor to her people. The spies promised Rehab that if she would hang a scarlet cord from her home, she and her father's house would be saved when Israel entered Jericho. After the walls of Jericho fell, Rehab lived out the rest of her life in Israel. She eventually married and became the mother to Boaz, the great grandfather of King David.

Similarly, we were born into a heritage of sin, but the revelation of Christ, should shake and stir us to the point that we are ready and willing to become a traitor to the realm we were born into and take on a new identity in Christ! We lay aside the garments that are stained with sin. We put to death the old man that is our sinful nature, and we are born again, raised to new life in the Spirit.

When God moved his people, Rehab's homeland was destroyed. There was nothing left for her there. When God calls us out of darkness and into his glorious light, there is nothing left for us in our old life. There is nothing to return to except for destruction.

Christ is described as the stone the builders rejected. In Romans he is referred to as a rock of offense, a stone that is stumbled on. When we are confronted with the saving knowledge of grace through Christ, we must make a decision. Will we accept that he is the only path forward, or will we reject him? Will we stumble? Or will we build?

To Rehab, Israel's invasion of her home was that encounter with the truth of a living God. She could stumble in her pride and die with her people, or she could act on the faith that had been born in her and build a new life with the people of God.

Imagine what would have happened, had Rehab decided to remain faithful to her heritage. Her future would have been one of death. Imagine what would have happened, if Rehab would have returned to the destruction of her old home. She would have faced death.

Instead, she acted on her faith, and continued to act on her faith. The heritage of destruction she was born into was laid aside, so she could become part of the heritage of the Lord!

Let's use today to look back on our testimony; the day we decided to build with Christ. Let's ask the Lord to stir our hearts, as we remember all he delivered us from. Let's commit to walk out that faith with new boldness, and act on the Word of God that has the power to change our lives and the lives of others. Commit today to turn your faith into action! You are not dead. You have been raised to new life in Christ!

WRAP

Choose a verse from today's reading, and follow the steps below.

Write the verse:	Reflect on its meaning:	Apply it to your life:	Pray about today's reading:

Notes & Questions:

Today's Big Idea

Faith without action looks a whole lot like being spiritually dead

Digging Deeper

Death of our old nature…

Romans 6:6 - our old nature was crucified with Christ, so that we'd be free from sin

Galatians 5:19-21 the fruit of the flesh

Ephesians 4:22 put off your old conduct

Raised to Life…

Romans 6:11 - when we count ourselves dead to sin, we are raised to life through Christ

Galatians 5:22-23 fruit of the Spirit

2 Corinthians 5:17 Anyone in Christ, is a new creature

Colossians 3:10 renewed in knowledge after the image of God

We are now the in the family of God…

John 1:12 receiving Christ, gives us the right to be God's children

Ephesians 2:19 we are members of God's household

1 John 3:2 we are now the sons of God

Romans 11:17 we (a wild branch), are grafted in, and partake of the root and the fatness of the olive tree, just like Israel.

Day 16

G1320 teachers

G5468 to restrain

G2917 the issue of judicial process

G3982 To persuade; urge

1 My brethren, be not many masters, knowing that we
shall receive the greater condemnation. 2 For in many
things we offend all. If any man offend not in word,
the same is a perfect man, and able also to bridle the
whole body. 3 Behold, we put bits in the horses'
mouths, that they may obey us and we turn their
whole body. 4 Behold also the ships, which though
they be so great, are driven of fierce winds, yet are they
turned about with a very small helm, wheresoever the
governor listeth. 5A Even so the tongue is a little
member, and boasteth great things.

G1014 be disposed, mended, intend, of own will

James 3: 1-5A

Directions: Respond to the prompts below.

1. What do you struggle with the most when it comes to controlling what you say?

2. How has a lack of self-control with words complicated things for you in the past?

3. Write a prayer asking God to help you recognize foolish words before they are spoken.

Daily Devotional

1 Samuel 25

After being anointed the future King of Israel, defeating Goliath, and proving himself to be skilled in combat, David is on the run from King Saul. Jealous of David's fame, Saul wanted David dead.

While on the run, David came in contact with shepherds that worked for Nabal. Nabal owned 3,000 sheep and 1,000 goats near Carmel. During David's time with them, he and his men provided protection for them. After the sheep had been sheared, and Nabal had his feast, David sent ten of his men to go speak with Nabal, and let him know that they had helped protect his possessions, which could be confirmed by Nabal's workers, and to see if they could partake in the feast.

Nabal had a reputation for being foolish, greedy, and unreasonable. In short, he responded to David's messengers with questions: Who's David? Who's the son of Jesse? Don't many people run from their masters? Why should I give up my resources to help?

In asking who David was, Nabal showed that he was either completely unaware of current events, or he was being disrespectful on purpose. When he compared David's run from Saul as a servant running from their master, he made it clear that he was in fact aware of current events. Granted, 600 men is a lot of people to feed, but responding with insults is probably not the best way to go about it. Especially, when you own 3,000 sheep, and 1,000 goats, and none of them were lost to wolves or thieves.

When the messengers returned to David, he was livid. He got together 400 men to kill Nabal and every man under his leadership. Today we focus on the guilt or innocence of the individual, but during this time period, focus was placed on community shame and honor. If you were a leader, everyone paid the price for your missteps. If you were not publicly shamed, then it was assumed your behavior was ok. In cultural context, if David let Nabal's actions go unanswered, his honor would be tarnished, and a precedent would be set. However, cultural norms should not be confused with God's will.

Meanwhile, the workers that overheard Nabal's conversation with David's messengers went straight to Abigail, Nabal's wife. Knowing exactly who David was, and that he would not stand for being insulted, they feared for their lives. They knew Abigail had wisdom, and could smooth things over.

Abigail loaded donkeys with enough food to feed all the men, and went out to meet David. She apologized for the foolish insults of her husband, and asked that he accept the gifts of their resources and extend mercy. She offered to bear the transgression of her husband.

David thanked God for sending her. He blessed her for her advice, for coming to keep him from shedding blood, and because she kept him from avenging himself with his own hand. Abigail went home and told her husband what she had done. At the news, Nabal's heart died within him, and he died ten days later. This was most likely a heart attack. God avenged David by taking out only the one deserving wrath.

In this story we see just how much words matter! We live in a time when it's funny to be disrespectful like Nabal. All this does is provoke wrath in others. Instead, we should seek to use our words wisely to smooth over situations like Abigail.

WRAP

Choose a verse from today's reading, and follow the steps below.

Write the verse:	Reflect on its meaning:	Apply it to your life:	Pray about today's reading:

Notes & Questions:

Today's Big Idea

Practice self-control with your words

Digging Deeper

Standards for leader…

Galatians 1:1 called by God, not man
1 Timothy 3:1-7 character & conduct honors Christ
Titus 1:9 has the ability to teach sound doctrine
1 Peter 5:3 leads by example, not by domineering others

Resolving Offences…

Matthew 18:15-17 follow the right order
Romans 12:17 do not repay evil for evil
Ephesians 4:2-3 be eager to maintain unity of the spirit

Proverbs for Watching our Words

Proverbs 10:19 when there are many words, transgression is unavoidable
Proverbs 11:12 anyone who belittles his neighbor lacks sense, a person of understanding holds his peace.
Proverbs 13:3 guarding what you say will preserve your life
Proverbs 21:23 those that are careful about what they say have fewer troubles

Day 17

G5208
forest, wood, fuel
possibly related to G3586

G93
injustice,
unrighteousness of
heart

G4695
To defile, spot; to stain
or soil

5B Behold, how great a matter a little fire
kindleth! 6 And the tongue is a fire, a world
of iniquity: so is the tongue among our
members, that it defileth the whole body,
and setteth on fire the course of nature; and
is set on fire of hell. 7 For every kind of
beasts, and of birds, and of serpents and of
things in the sea, is tamed, and hath been
tamed of mankind: 8 But the tongue can no
man tame; it is an unruly evil, full of deadly
poison.

James 3: 5B-8

Directions: Respond to the prompts below.

1. Describe a time that expressing your feelings, turned a little flame into raging fire?

2. How could you have better handled the situation? What lessons have you learned?

Daily Devotional

Philippians 4:2-3 & Matthew 18: 15-17

Euodia and Syntyche are only mentioned briefly at the end of Paul's letter to the Philippians. Paul urges the two women to come into unity with the Lord. We aren't told why they had a falling out, but we can infer that it was most likely quite public for Paul to have heard about the argument from prison.

We also know that these women were believers who actively participated in ministry, Paul follows up at the end of verse 3 stating that their names are written in the book of life. Just because believers wind up in conflict does not mean that one or the other is unsaved, simply that at this moment they are not acting in unity with God. This doesn't erase their name from the book of life, but it does greatly impair the ministry that God is trying to accomplish. If conflict continues unresolved, sins such as pride and strife will enter the situation and wreak havoc for everyone aware of the problem.

Conflicts will happen among believers. When they do, we must be careful. A little issue between a few people can sweep through the whole church like a forest fire. In these moments we tend to give into our flesh nature, involving ourselves unnecessarily. This only makes the situation worse, and hurts many people in the process.

If someone at church has wronged you, it is important to follow the biblical order that Christ lays out for us in Matthew to resolve problems quickly and correctly. First, we should go directly to our brother or sister in Christ and try to come to a resolution, using the Bible as our guide. Next, each party should come together with a couple witnesses to try and bring a resolution. This is not a time for each group to gang up on the other group, but rather all parties should aim to seek truth and restoration in love. Finally, if the problem cannot be resolved, then all involved parties should bring the matter before the church for a final decision to be made on the matter. This process will start by involving the pastor, and following his lead.

Back biting and spreading gossip are never the right answer, and will not bring resolution to a situation. Instead, it will sow division and discord among the congregation. How many church splits could have been avoided had people not given a place to gossip?

The best things we can do when we know about contention among fellow believers is pray for God to bring wisdom and discernment into the situation, encourage reconciliation, refuse to listen to disparaging remarks, and inform church leadership if reconciliation seems unlikely without intervention.

In Psalms 141:3 David asked the Lord to set a guard over his mouth, and watch the door of his lips. Let this also be our prayer.

WRAP

Choose a verse from today's reading, and follow the steps below.

Write the verse:	Reflect on its meaning:	Apply it to your life:	Pray about today's reading:

Notes & Questions:

Today's Big Idea

Be mindful of your words, so that you don't create forest fires!

Digging Deeper

Resolving Conflict…

Proverbs 15:1 a soft word will turn away wrath

Ephesians 4:31-32 put away bitterness, wrath, slander, and choose to be kind, tenderhearted and forgiving.

Colossians 3:13 make room for one another's faults

Watch your Words…

Proverbs 15:4 words can give life or crush the spirit

Ephesians 4:29 speak things that are helpful to build up the church

1 Peter 3:10 if you love life keep your tongue in check

Day 18

G2127
to praise, to speak well of

G2532
and, even, also, namely

G3669
likeness

G1831
To go or come out of

[9] Therewith bless we God even the Father;
and therewith curse we men, which are
made after the similitude of God. [10] Out of
the same mouth proceedeth blessing and
cursing. My brethren, these things ought
not so to be. [11] Doth a fountain send forth at
the same place sweet water and bitter? [12]
Can the fig tree, my brethren bear olive
berries? Either a vine figs? So can no
fountain both yield salt water and fresh.

James 3: 9-12

Directions: Respond to the prompts below.

1. Describe a time that you used your words to show Christ to others.

2. Describe a time you did not show Christ to others with your words.

3. Compare the end result of both situations.

Daily Devotional

2 Kings 2:19-22

Early in Elisha's ministry, he was called upon to help a community whose water had become harmful to them. As a result, the land was now barren. Elisha called for a new cruse to be filled with salt. He took the cruse to the waters, dumped the salt in, and said the waters were healed, and they were healed.

In Matthew 5, Christ calls us to be the salt of the earth. Salt is an interesting substance. It adds flavor, preserves, heals, and makes fires burn brighter. Salt is formed by a chemical reaction between Sodium and Chloride. This ionic bond forms when Sodium shares its extra electron with Chloride, which is lacking an electron. Sodium is powerfully explosive in nature. Chlorine is a deadly gas. When they come together a new substance is created; salt! When we eat salt, the bond is broken. The lethal chlorine evaporates, but the flavor of the sodium is left behind.

Likewise, Jesus is so powerful all on his own! We are dead in our sin, but an interaction with Christ changes us forever. He fills all the gaps where we are lacking. When we come into contact with other people the flavor left behind should be that of Christ.

If you've spent much time in the south, you've probably heard the phrase, "that person made me lose my religion!" So many times, when communicating with others, we let the toxicity of our flesh be the impression that is left behind. We must learn self-control, so that we are representing Christ and the work he has done in us, rather than ourselves.

With the help of Christ, we can be salt that brings healing, preservation, good flavor, and a brighter light to the world. But we must learn to be mindful of the words we speak. Like James teaches us today, it should not be that both blessings and curses are coming from the same mouth. As followers of Christ, we should bear the fruit of Christ.

WRAP

Choose a verse from today's reading, and follow the steps below.

Write the verse:	Reflect on its meaning:	Apply it to your life:	Pray about today's reading:

Notes & Questions:

Today's Big Idea

Make sure your talk is reflecting your walk

Digging Deeper

The Importance of our Words...

Proverbs 18:21 death and life are in the power of the tongue

Matthew 12:37 by your words you will be justified or condemned.

Matthew 15:8 the words you speak started in your heart

Bearing Good Fruit (shows up in our Speech) …

Matthew 7:17-20 the fruit you bear is reflective of your (spiritual) health

Luke 3:8 is a sign of repentance

John 15:8 glorifies God, and shows that we are disciples of Christ.

Day 19

G4680
skilled, learned, cultivated, clever

G1990
intelligent; ability

G391
behavior, conduct

G4678
Skill, wisdom; insight skill (human or devine)

G2052
contention, contentious, strife; *self-seeking*

13 Who is a wise man and endued with
knowledge among you? Let him shew out of
a good conversation his works with
meekness of wisdom. 14 But if ye have bitter
envying and strife in your hearts, glory not,
and lie not against the truth. 15 This wisdom
descendeth not from above, but is earthly,
sensual, devilish. 16 For where envying and
strife is, there is confusion and every evil
work.

James 3: 13-16

Directions: Respond to the prompts below.

1. Today we looked at one aspect of worldly wisdom: Profiting off of God's gifts. What other examples can you think of where the wisdom of God is substituted with that of the world?

2. Describe a time you followed the world's wisdom, even though you knew God's wisdom.

3. How did this substitution affect your walk with God?

Daily Devotional

2 Kings 5

After invading Israel, one captive girl was taken to serve the wife of Naaman, the commander over Aram's army. Naaman was plagued with leprosy, so the girl informed Naaman's wife that if he'd go to Israel and visit the prophet Elisha, he could be healed.

With permission from his King, Naaman was sent with a letter and treasure to the King of Israel to be healed. The King thought it was a trap to pick a fight, but Elisha sent word for the king to send Naaman so that he would know there was a true prophet in Israel.

Naaman expected Elisha to come out and greet him with a fuss, wave his hands as the magicians do. He probably thought Elisha would get loud or speak fancy words, summoning his god in the way people do to draw attention to themselves. He was sorely disappointed when Elisha didn't do any of that.

Elisha sent a messenger with a simple message: Go wash in the Jordan river seven times. Your skin will be healed, and you'll be clean.

Naaman was offended. The Jordan River was filthy. He felt his time had been wasted, but his servant pointed out that had Elisha told him to do something hard he would have. So Naaman obeyed and was healed.

He returned to Elisha, getting an introduction this time! Praised the Lord for his healing and said that he would never praise any other god than the God of Israel. He urged Elisha to take the treasures he had brought in exchange for his healing, but Elisha refused.

After Naaman left, Elisha's servant Gehazi went after Naaman and said that some of the treasure was needed after all. Naaman gladly gave Gehazi twice what he asked for, and Gehazi took the treasure back and hid it in his house.

When Gehazi saw Elisha later he was confronted for his sin. Because of his actions, Gehazi and his family were cursed with the Leprosy of Naaman.

Unlike Gehazi, Elisha had the wisdom of the Lord, and he knew the gifts of God are not for sale. Gehazi, consumed in the wisdom of this world, thought Elisha a fool. Seeking his own self-interests, he conducted himself poorly. The take away for Naaman was supposed to be that, even as someone born outside of God's covenant, he could come to God freely and receive healing. He could change his beliefs, and worship the Lord. While Naaman willingly gave to Gehazi, imagine the confusion this could have caused. This would not just cause confusion between Elisha's words and Gehazi's, but also about the very nature of God.

We too are susceptible to fall for the same trap Gehazi fell into, where he prized the wisdom of the world over the wisdom of God. Even Simon the Sorcerer in Acts 8, came to believe in Christ, but missed in this area of thinking that the gifts of God could be sold. Peter heavily rebuked Simon for this belief, and told him he could have no part in ministry. Substituting the wisdom of God for the wisdom of the world is dangerous business for the believer.

Guarding against this starts with having reverence for God. The fear of the Lord is the beginning of Wisdom [Psalm 111:10]. To be wise we must revere God as holy, and do away with character flaws like jealousy and bitterness that would prompt us to exalt our interests above the interests of God.

WRAP

Choose a verse from today's reading, and follow the steps below.

Write the verse:

Reflect on its meaning:

Apply it to your life:

Pray about today's reading:

Notes & Questions:

Digging Deeper

Heavenly wisdom…

Job 28:12-13 is not found among the living
Job 28: 15-19 cannot be bought
Job 28:27 God has prepared it and examined it
Job 28:28 God declares to man that fearing him is wisdom
heavenly wisdom starts with having reverence for the Lord

Worldly Wisdom…

Genesis 3:6-7 leads to sin
Proverbs 16:25 leads to death
Romans 1:21-22 will turn you into a fool
It will cause you to substitute the glory of the Living God, for idols you create yourself
1 Corinthians 3:19 is foolish before God, you'll stumble over it and be trapped by it.

Christian Conduct…

Colossians 1:10 walk worthy of God, fully pleasing, bearing fruit, and increasing our knowledge of God
Titus 3:2 avoid arguing and be courteous
Philippians 4:8 think on things that honor Christ

Today's Big Idea

Be careful not to substitute God's wisdom with the wisdom of the world

Day 20

G2138
easily obeyed, compliant

17 But the wisdom that is from above is first pure, then peaceable, gentle, and easy to be entreated, full of mercy and good fruits, without partiality, and without hypocrisy.
18 And the fruit of righteousness is sown in peace of them that make peace.

James 3: 17-18

Directions: Respond to the prompts below.

1. What characteristics of God's wisdom are an encouragement to you?

2. What is one way you can seek God's wisdom this week?

Daily Devotional

Daniel 1:3-21

Daniel's story begins in his teen years as an exile taken to Babylon. Once there, he would go through three years of training to be placed in the Babylonian King's service. When Daniel and his companions arrive, they are presented with the best food that Babylon has to offer. A conflict arises when Daniel is unwilling to defile his body with unclean meat and the king's wine.

The prince of the eunuchs was in charge of carrying for all the young men. Daniel respectfully asked if it would be possible that he not defile himself with these items. Though the Eunuch was worried about the Kings opinions, he had favor on Daniel and granted the four children of Judah a 10-day experiment to eat only pulse (legumes and grains), water, and possibly herbs.

At the end of the ten days, they were in better health than all the other children under the eunuch's care. God blessed them with knowledge, skill for learning, and wisdom.

Throughout Daniel's life, he exemplified divine wisdom in action. Regardless of the political circumstances around him, he continuously and graciously honored God. His life bore the fruit of righteousness, and he lived peaceably fulfilling his duties to the Babylonian King.

Humility is often mistaken for weakness, but to those that serve the Lord it is a great strength. Daniel never compromised his beliefs. When a law was passed that forbid him from praying, he did it anyway, and in the same manner he always had before. This decision landed him in a den with some starving lions, but the Lord was faithful to Daniel and sent angels to shut the mouths of the lions, and they did not attack Daniel.

Sometimes, we get caught up in clever wisdom: perfectly stated and timed words that provoke deep thought. We all benefit from practical wisdom that leads to a profitable life. Daniel had divine wisdom that comes from the Lord and leads to all other types of wisdom and knowledge. Applying this wisdom keeps us in the center of God's will, exhibits the fruits of the spirit, and draws others to the Lord.

In James chapter 1, we read that God gives wisdom abundantly to all who ask for it. Proverbs communicates that wisdom starts with respecting God. God desires for us to be wise and to know him. He communicates the intent of his heart throughout his word. Throughout his word, he teaches us sound doctrine, so that we can live victoriously.

We do not have to live this life as fools. We can choose to live with wisdom!

WRAP

Choose a verse from today's reading, and follow the steps below.

Write the verse:

Reflect on its meaning:

Apply it to your life:

Pray about today's reading:

Notes & Questions:

Today's Big Idea

Seek the divine wisdom of the Lord.

Digging Deeper

The fruit of the spirit

Galatians 5:22-23 love, joy, peace, patience, kindness, goodness, faithfulness, gentleness, self-control

1 Corinthians 13 Characteristics of love

The fruit of the flesh

Galatians 5:19-21 adultery, fornication, uncleanness, lasciviousness, idolatry, hatred, variance, emulations, wrath, strife, seditions, heresies, envyings, murders, drunkenness, and revellings

Hypocrites

Matthew 6:16-18 have received their reward on earth

Matthew 23:27-28 are like whitewashed tombs that look good on the outside but are full of dead bones

Luke 20:46-47 devour the weak

Galatians 6:3 deceive themselves

Titus 1:16 are unfit for good work

Day 21

G1782
from this place

G3196
limbs

G2372
long for, covet, desire

1 From whence come wars and fightings
among you? Come they not hence, even of
your lusts that war in your members? 2 Ye
lust, and have not: ye kill, and desire to have,
and cannot obtain: ye fight and war, yet ye
have not because ye ask not. 3 Ye ask and
receive not, because ye ask amiss, that ye
may consume it upon your lusts.

G2560
badly(physical or moral), amiss, evil, grievously, miserably; improperly, wrongly

James 4: 1-3

Directions: Consider the current state of your prayer life, and answer the questions below.

1. What causes you to fight/argue with others?

2. What causes you to fight/argue within yourself?

3. What solutions does James offer to bring an end to the turmoil in your life?

Daily Devotional

Numbers 16:1-35

Conflict stems from unmet needs or desires in one or more involved parties. When our hearts are not aligned with the heart of God, unchecked desires can lead to poor behavior and conflict.

Consider Korah, a leader among the Levites, tasked with the transportation of holy items in the tabernacle as they traveled through the desert to the promised land. Korah had the amazing privilege of being one of the people who could touch the ark of the covenant when it needed to be moved without being struck dead.

Sadly, Korah did not see the honor in this possession. Overcome by jealousy towards Moses and Aaron for their positions of leadership, he incited a rebellion with Dathan and Abiram, as well as 250 other leaders of Israel. He went to Moses and argued that since all of Israel had been set apart by God as his chosen people, then any Israelite should be able to lead.

Moses reasoned with Korah that the following day all the rebels would come out and burn incense before the Lord and Aaron would also bring an incense burner, and the Lord would receive the offering from His holy one. Before ending the conversation, Moses urged Korah to see the honor in his position, that among all the Israelites, God would choose Korah to be so close to God's very presence.

The problem was that Korah didn't care about being near to God's presence. Korah cared about power.

When Moses called to Dathan and Abiram, they refused to come. They accused Moses of bringing them into the desert to die. They whined that they had a land of milk and honey in Egypt, and they had yet to make it to another land with milk and honey, nor did they have fields or vineyards.

The following day Korah, Dathan, Abiram, and their 250 followers came with their incense burners. Additionally, Korah had stirred up the whole community, so they all came to watch.

Then God's presence appeared before the whole community. The Lord told Moses and Arron to get away from the people because God was going to destroy everyone that was near Korah and his followers. Moses, urged people to move away so that they would not incur the consequences of God's wrath. Then God opened the earth, burying Korah, Dathan, Abiram, and their families alive with all their belongings. Then God sent fire from heaven to consume the 250 rebels who came with their incense burners.

God has a plan for each of us. He wants to use us in a special and unique way. He desires to answer our prayers. James points out that we have not because we ask not. A person who isn't asking, is most likely not taking time to pray or enter God's presence. When we desire power more than the presence of God, we cannot be surprised that our prayers go unanswered. When we let our desires go unchecked and turn into covetousness towards others we can't be surprised when our life is filled with fighting and war.

We may not get swallowed up by the earth for our disobedience, but unchecked desires can wreak havoc on a church. When people are more concerned for their agendas, positions, and notoriety than they are for the heart of God, people always get hurt.

WRAP

Choose a verse from today's reading, and follow the steps below.

Write the verse:	Reflect on its meaning:	Apply it to your life:	Pray about today's reading:

Notes & Questions:

Today's Big Idea

*Line up your heart with God's heart

*Check your motive when asking God for your desires

Digging Deeper

Common Causes of Strife

Proverbs 13:10 insolence (i.e., disrespectful behavior)
Proverbs 15:18 a hot temper
Proverbs 16:28 dishonesty and gossip
Proverbs 28:25 greed

Pursue Peace

Proverbs 12:20 You'll have joy in your heart
Romans 12:17-19 God is the judge and jury
Romans 14:19 It builds one another up

Time in prayer...

Psalms 107:28 brings deliverance
Matthew 26:41 strengthens the body against temptation
Ephesians 6:18-20 strengthens the church for ministry
Philippians 4:6-7 combats anxiety
James 5:14-16 brings healing

Day 22

4 Ye adulterers and adulteresses, know ye not that the friendship of the world is enmity
with God? Whosoever therefore will be a friend of the world is the enemy of God. 5 Do ye
think that the scripture saith in vain, the spirit that dwelleth in us lusteth to envy? 6 But
he giveth more grace. Wherefore he saith, God resisteth the proud, but giveth grace unto
the humble. 7 Submit yourselves therefore to God. Resist the devil, and he will flee from
you. 8 Draw nigh to God, and he will draw nigh to you. Cleanse your hands, ye sinners:
and purify your hearts, ye double minded. 9 Be afflicted, and mourn and weep: let your
laughter be turned to mourning, and your joy to heaviness. 10 Humble yourselves in the
sight of the lord, and he shall lift you up.

James 4:4-10

G2189
hostility, a reason for implication - hatred

G2889
dear, friend; actively, fond, friendly

G2761
To no purpose

G5293
to subordinate; reflexively, to obey

G1448
to make near reflexively, approach, be at hand

G5003
to be wretched; to realize one's own misery

G5013
to depress; figuratively, to humiliate (in condition or heart), bring low, humble

Directions: Think about a sin that you have been redeemed from. Journal prayer of thanks/repentance to God for his redeeming love in your life.

Daily Devotional

Hosea 1-3

The story of Hosea was written to show God's unfailing love for us. In marrying Gomer, Hosea brought her out of the shameful life of prostitution, and gave her a place of honor as a wife and mother. Perhaps it was due to emotional wounds, personal insecurities, or desire for the excitement of her old life. We don't know exactly why, but Gomer left her husband to return to prostitution. After a season of separation, God instructed Hosea to go and buy Gomer back. Under the law, he should have stoned her, but he paid to get her back, and was reconciled with her.

Like Gomer, we have been redeemed from our past by God. Our chains are gone and we are washed white as snow. As the bride of Christ our lives have been changed from dishonorable to honorable. Even so, we often fall prey to our emotions and the longings of our flesh, and follow our feelings back to our former bondage. One can easily imagine how Hosea likely felt when Gomer left him for her former life, those feelings of anger, confusion, and heartbreak mirror the feelings God has towards us when we choose to partake in our favorite sins.

In Hosea 2 God outlines that eventually, Israel will recognize that they had things better serving the Lord and return to him, just like an adulterous wife would. This is sadly the cycle that many Christians never escape, being a yo-yo caught between bondage and redemption. However, God's plan for our life is always one of freedom and reconciliation with him.

The story of Gomer confirms Jeremiah's words that the heart is deceitful above all things, and desperately wicked [Jer. 17:9]. We're often told to follow our hearts, but it's the lust of our heart's that will lead to our bondage and destruction. Rather than our hearts, we should follow Christ. He is the path to life!

WRAP

Choose a verse from today's reading, and follow the steps below.

Write the verse:	Reflect on its meaning:	Apply it to your life:	Pray about today's reading:

Notes & Questions:

Today's Big Idea

*The lust of our flesh will lead us astray, but the Grace of God is so much greater.

*God's plans for us are good, and he is worthy of our submission.

Digging Deeper

Our relationship with the world

Romans 12:2 we should not conform to it

1 John 3:13 we should not be surprised when the world hates us

1 John 5:19 the world lies in wickedness

God's Great Grace

Romans 3:24 saves us from the penalty of Sin

Acts 20:24 should be testified of

2 Corinthians 9:8 enables us to do the work God has called us to

Ephesians 4:7; 2 Corinthians 12:9; 1 Peter 4:10

Returning to Sin after Repentance

Romans 6:1-2 We shouldn't continue in sin because grace is here. How can we live like that? we're dead to sin.

John 5:14 returning to sin after being made whole, can open the door for worse things in your life

2 Peter 2:20-22; Luke 11: 24-26

1John 1:9 if you sin, repent

Draw near to God

Psalm 65:4 you will be satisfied in his presence

James 4:8 he will draw near to you

Hebrews 4:16 you will find mercy and grace

Day 23

G2919 to judge, decide; judge in court of law or privately
G2635 speak evil; rail, slander
G2923 a judge; magistrate, ruler

11 Speak not evil one of another, brethren.
He that speaketh evil of his brother, judgeth
his brother, speaketh evil of the law, and
judgeth the law: but if thou judge the law,
thou art not a doer of the law, but a judge.
12 There is one lawgiver, who is able to save
and to destroy: who art thou that judges
another?

James 4: 11-12

Directions: Respond to the prompts below.

1. Describe a time you passed judgement on someone without knowing their story.

2. Describe a time you decided not to share the gospel with someone? What was your motive?

3. In these scenarios how were your feelings towards God impacted? How was your overall mood affected by your actions?

Daily Devotional

Jonah 1-4

God called Jonah to preach in Nineveh that God would destroy their city unless they repent. Nineveh was the capital city of Israel's enemy. God's act of mercy towards Nineveh shows us that even before Christ, God desired a relationship with all people. He was ready and willing to extend his mercy to anyone that would repent of sin and obey him.

Jonah looked at Nineveh as though they were scum, worthy of destruction. Rather than focusing on obeying God's word, he thought himself superior enough to judge God's word. Jonah believed that he had the right to determine who was worthy of salvation or destruction.

Self-righteous Jonah decided to hop on a boat and go the opposite direction. I suppose he thought that once he landed somewhere new, God would forget about Nineveh and call him to a new task. The thing is, we can't do the work of God without the help of God. At the same time, God won't readily give up on using us to complete what he wants done.

Jonah wound up thrown overboard on a stormy sea, and then swallowed by a big fish. This is my favorite part of the story! The last verse of chapter 1 says that Jonah was in the fish for 3 days and 3 nights. Chapter 2, verse 1 says, ***"THEN"*** he prayed! Every child story depicts Jonah praying to God for three days and three nights, until finally God hears him and acts. The bible shows us that Jonah remained rebellious, in the disgusting belly of a fish, preserved from death by God, for 3 days before he finally decided that maybe, just maybe, he should obey God's command, rather than judging it. God answered Jonah's prayer of repentance immediately.

After preaching to Nineveh, the entire city held a fast and repented. They turned to God, and they were spared. This made Jonah angry. He just did not feel they deserved God's grace. In chapter 4, God shows Jonah that he had more compassion for a plant than he did for human beings.

Sometimes, we can be like Jonah too! We make judgements about people without knowing anything about their life. We judge them personally for their sin without knowing whether or not they have a relationship with Christ. Sinners aren't sinners because of their sin. We are all born into sin, and remain in sin until we are raised to life in Christ. Sinners sin because they're still sinners. Life is not in them.

Yet, we determine ahead of time whether or not people are worthy of the gospel. Determining their value is not our job. God already determined their value. God already declared them worthy of the call to repentance. Our job is to obey the command. Their job is to decide how they will respond.

In today's passage, we're instructed that our job is to do the law. When we judge others, we judge the law. The only person holy enough to judge the law, is the one that gave the law: God.

This may seem contradictory to scripture that instruct us to expose evil and restore others to Christ when they fall into sin. The issue at hand is not judgment, but motive. Righteous judgement is motivated by love to expose wickedness for the purpose of restoring others to Christ.

To our brothers in Christ, we should seek to restore. To the lost, we should seek to share the gospel. Both should be done in love. Any other motive is unprofitable.

WRAP

Choose a verse from today's reading, and follow the steps below.

Write the verse:	Reflect on its meaning:	Apply it to your life:	Pray about today's reading:

Notes & Questions:

Today's Big Idea

Focus on obeying God's word

Digging Deeper

Overcoming Evil with Good

Matthew 5:9 peacemakers are called sons of God
Luke 6:35 you will be rewarded
Romans 12:20-21 is like putting a heap of coals on your enemy
Proverbs 25:21-22
Romans 13:10 love does no wrong to others

Speaking Or Doing Evil Towards Others…

Psalm 101:3-5 will bring destruction
Malachi 2:10 profanes the covenant God has with his people
Titus 1:15-16 makes one worthless of any good work
Matthew 7:1-2 brings judgment by the same standard

The Call to Share the Gospel…

Mark 13:10 the gospel must be proclaimed to all nations
Mark 16:15-20 The lord works with us, and confirms his word
Luke 10:2 pray for more laborers to help in the harvest
Acts 1:8 The holy spirit empowers us to do the work

Day 24

G71
to lead, bring, carry; guide, go, come

G4160
to make, do; act, spend

G1710
to travel, to traffic by implication of trade; engage in trade as a merchant

G2309
to will, wish; intend design, wish, desire

G212
boastfulness; show, arrogant display

13 Go to now, ye that say, Today or
tomorrow we will go into such a city, and
continue there a year, and buy and sell, and
get gain: 14 Whereas ye know not what shall
be on the morrow. For what is your life? It
is even a vapour, that appeareth for a little
time, and then vanisheth away. 15 For that
ye ought to say, if the Lord will, we shall
live, and do this, or that. 16 But now ye rejoice
in your boastings: all such rejoicing is evil. 17
Therefore to him that knoweth to do good,
and doeth it not, to him it is sin.

James 4: 13-17

Directions: Respond to the prompts below.

1. Which of the areas mentioned in the reading cause you the most worry? Or take up the most mental space?

2. Ask God to help you trust him more in this area of your life, and create a plan for when this worry shows up.

Daily Devotional

Luke 12:13-34

The parable of the rich fool tells the story of a man who owned a fertile farm. His land produced so many crops that he didn't have room to store it all. He thought to himself that he would tear down all his barns and build back bigger! Then, when all his store houses were full, he would retire. He'd eat, drink, and be merry, knowing that he had provision to last him several years.

God spoke, and called the man a fool, saying he would die that same night! And God asked him who would get everything this man worked so hard to build.

Then Jesus taught his followers that we shouldn't worry about everyday life. While food and clothing are important, life is about more than that. If God provides for the birds, how much more would he take care of us? We're much more valuable to God than the birds! The same goes for the flowers and all of creation. Spending our time worrying over our provisions won't make them appear, but God will see to it that we are provided for.

Rather than seeking wealth and a life of ease, we should start by seeking the Lord!

Most likely, we've all been as guilty as the rich fool, planning our future without consulting God. We've probably all worried about having enough provisions at least once in our life, or fallen into the trap of feeling inadequate by comparison. All of these things lead to worry and can put us in a perpetual state of anxiety.

There's nothing wrong with being prepared. The woman described in Proverbs 31 has no fear of winter because her children's clothes are prepared, and her stores are full. To never prepare for anything would be foolish. However, living our whole life consumed by far out preparations leaves little time for the Lord. Time spent with our heads in the clouds dreaming or worrying, results in a lack of productivity right now. Having our goals set in stone, doesn't leave room for God to inspire us with the plans he has in mind for our life. When our goals don't pan out on the time schedules we planned, we become weary in unmet expectations. We judge ourselves as failures, and compare our material successes to that of others. All the while, we're missing out on so much growth that we could have had in the Lord, and we're missing out on the dreams and timeline that he has planned for us.

Our life is a vapor. It won't last forever. The best way to make the most of it, is to put God first in it!

WRAP

Choose a verse from today's reading, and follow the steps below.

Write the verse:	Reflect on its meaning:	Apply it to your life:	Pray about today's reading:

Notes & Questions:

Today's Big Idea

Let God plan your future

Digging Deeper

Planning for the future the right way

Proverbs 16:3 Commit your work to the Lord, and your plans will be established

Proverbs 20:18 Seek wise counsel

Proverbs 21:5 be diligent in your planning, hastiness leads to poverty

Don't let fear paralyze you!

Romans 8:28 God works all things for good

Colossians 3:23 do all your work, as if you're doing it for God

1 Timothy 5:8 you have to provide for your family

sometimes we feel immobilized by our fear of making the wrong choice for our future. Don't get caught up in that. Go to work, and commit it all to God. He knows your heart, and he'll sort it all out.

Philippians 1:6 God is going to finish the work he started in you

Planning for the future the wrong way…

Proverbs 15:22 Plans lacking counsel fail

Proverbs 19:21 Plans made without God fail

Psalms 9:16 Wicked plans will eventually backfire

Other stories of planning

Genesis 41 Joseph prepares Egypt for Famine

Joshua 5&6 Joshua plans with God to face Jericho

Joshua 7 Joshua uses his own plan to face Ai

Proverbs 31 The preparations of a good woman

Day 25

1 Go to now, ye rich men, weep and howl for your miseries that shall come upon you. 2 Your
riches are corrupted, and your garments are motheaten. 3 Your gold and silver is cankered; and
the rust of them shall be a witness against you, and shall eat your flesh as it were fire. Ye have
heaped treasure together for the last days. 4 Behold, the hire of the labourers who have reaped
down your fields, which is of you kept back by fraud, crieth: and the cries of them which have
reaped are entered into the ears of the lord of Sabaoth. 5 Ye have lived in pleasure on the earth,
and been wanton; ye have nourished your hearts as in a day of slaughter. 6 Ye have condemned
and killed the just; and he doth not resist you.

James 5:1-6

G3649
to cry aloud; howl, lament, bewail

G4595
to corrupt; to rot

Special Note
Some versions translate verse 2-3 to say that the wealth you depended on will consume you

G4684
to live riotously; extravagantly

G5004
hard work, hardship, distress; misery, distress, toil

G2728
to rust over, tarnished

G4442
fire; heat of the sun

G5171
to live a luxurious life, live self-indulgently

Special Note
"Nourishing your hearts as in the day of slaughter" references the feasts that land owners would have at the time of harvest or slaughtering livestock James compares this to the treatment of the righteous and those that celebrate their condemnation.

Directions: Respond to the prompts below

1. Describe a time in your Christian walk where you related with some aspect of the church in Laodicea or those James is writing to.

2. How did you get back on the right track?

3. What are some things you can do to prevent yourself from backsliding into this state in the future?

Daily Devotional

Revelations 3:14-22

During the Roman Empire, Laodicea was a wealthy city, located on a trade route. It was also a center for industry and banking. In the book of Revelation, Christ rebukes the church of Laodicea in hope that some would repent and return to a relationship with him. He first chastises them for their claim of wealth. Though they have monetary wealth they are spiritually bankrupt. They are miserable, poor, blind, and naked, and they don't even realize it. Christ urges this church to buy gold, garments, and ointment from him. He says that his gold is purified and tried by fire, his white garments can be worn without shame, and the ointment will restore their sight. Jesus tells them, that he is standing on the outside of this church, knocking on the door. If someone would answer, he'd come in and have fellowship with them again.

Laodicea is often compared to the modern churches of the west. In America, we have been granted religious liberty in a way that no other country enjoys. We enjoy wealth and influence throughout the world, but in recent years we have become more consumed with comfort than we are with being the church. As the church, we should be sharing the gospel, and the gospel should be changing the culture. Instead, we counted the world as a misunderstood friend, and created an unholy mixture, which has diluted the power of the church. Often times, we are not hot or cold, but lukewarm and complacent. We pursue our sinful desires, and often conduct ourselves in a worse manner than the world. Church services glorify self and ignore the mission of Christ. The people do not notice that Jesus has left the building, and is now knocking to be invited back in to his own house.

Whether looking at the passage in James, Christ's words to Laodicea, or the modern church, the answer for the problem is the same: Open the door to Christ, repent and follow his lead. Where our heart is, our treasure is also. Let's make sure that we define our wealth by the standards of Christ, rather than the world.

WRAP

Choose a verse from today's reading, and follow the steps below.

Write the verse:

Reflect on its meaning:

Apply it to your life:

Pray about today's reading:

Notes & Questions:

Digging Deeper

Beware of Corruption in the Church

Isaiah 1:4 God turns his back on the corrupt

Galatians 6:8 stems from sowing to the flesh; likewise sowing to the spirit reaps eternal life.

2 Timothy 3:15 has an outward form of godliness, but denies the power of God

2 Peter 2:15 they love to gain from wrong doing

2 Peter 2:19 false teachers promise freedom, but are enslaved to corruption

Today's Big Idea

Wealth of the world is corruptible

Spiritual Wealth is only obtained through Christ

Day 26

7 Be patient therefore, brethren, unto the
coming of the Lord. Behold, the
husbandman waiteth for the precious fruit
of the earth, and hath long patience for it,
until he receive the early and latter rain.
8 Be ye also patient; stablish your hearts: for the
coming of the Lord draweth nigh.
9 grudge not one against another, brethren, lest ye be
condemned: behold, the judge standeth
before the door.

James 5: 7-9

G1092 vinedresser; worker of the soil, farmer, farm-laborer

G4741 to make fast, establish; fix firmly, support, strengthen

G4727 groan; expressing grief, anger

G2443 and G3361 two words together mean to prevent; so that you will not

Directions: Respond to the prompts below.

1. What can you do to keep your lamp full in your walk with God?

2. How can you identify that you're starting to fall asleep spiritually?

3. How can you keep your lamp full when life gets chaotic?

Daily Devotional

Matthew 25:1-13

The parable of the 10 virgins opens in the context of a Jewish wedding. During this period, the bride and her bridesmaids would wait for the groom with their lamps lit. When the groom would come, the bridesmaids would light the way, as the bride and groom made their way to the groom's home for the wedding feast.

In the parable the groom is delayed in coming to retrieve his bride, so the bridesmaids had to wait longer than usual for him to arrive. In their waiting, they fell asleep. When the groom does come around midnight, the 10 young women realize they need to add more oil to their lamps. The wise virgins had oil, but the foolish virgins did not.

Once the foolish virgins bought oil, and came to the wedding feast, they found that the door had been shut. The groom came and told them that they could not enter the feast; he did not know them.

This parable is symbolic of Christ's second coming, and how we are to occupy the time while we wait for his return. The bridesmaids had the important job of shining their light. It is disputed whether the oil in the lamp represents salvation itself or a cultivated relationship with Christ through the holy spirit. It is Christ that redeems us, and the Holy spirit that empowers us to shine brightly in this world. Either way, we as the church are called to shine our light for the Lord.

As the groom's delay continued, all 10 of the young women fell asleep. As believers we have all had times in our lives where we have fallen asleep in our walk with the Lord. It doesn't take long to get caught up in our busy schedules or weighed down by the unmet expectations of life. Before we know it, our walk with God has greatly suffered, or even diminished into a back slidden state.

2 Peter 3:10 states that when Jesus returns it will be at an unexpected hour, like a thief in the night. Similarly, the midnight call of the groom's return was unexpected. It was at this time that the 10 young women realize their lanterns were running low on oil. The 5 foolish virgins did not bring enough oil for the long wait, and wanted the wise virgins to share. But we can't share our salvation or our walk with God with someone else. We can tell them how to obtain it for themselves, but it can't be given by man.

This is an ominous warning to believers. At the beginning of this story all 10 had oil in their lamp, but through a season of slumber, 5 lost what they had started with. At the end of the story, it was too late. The door was already shut. Similarly in the days of Noah, there were many years while Noah was building the ark for the people to repent. 2 Peter tells us that Noah preached righteousness to the people, but no one listened. Once the door was shut, it was too late.

There is a time for each of us when it is too late to return to God, whether that be closing our eyes in death, or the midnight call of Christ's return. It is important that we take the words of James to heart. We must use our time on earth to establish our hearts towards the Lord, because the time of the Lord draws more near each day.

WRAP

Choose a verse from today's reading, and follow the steps below.

Write the verse:	Reflect on its meaning:	Apply it to your life:	Pray about today's reading:

Notes & Questions:

Today's Big Idea

Keep your lamp full!

Digging Deeper

You Might Be Spiritually Asleep If...

Galatians 5:19-21 you're producing the fruit of the flesh

Ephesians 5:14-17 you're mistaken as being part of the world (spiritually dead)

1 Timothy 4:3-4 you will only tolerate teaching that flatters you

Wake Up! Be Alert!

Romans 13:11-12 our salvation is near

Ephesians 5:14 Wake up! Christ will give you light

1Peter 5:8 the devil is seeking whom he may devour

Day 27

G4396
a prophet; a person gifted at expositing divine truth

G2552
affliction; experience of evil, distress,

G3106
to bless; pronounce blessed

G4184
very compassionate

G3660
to swear, take an oath; promise with an oath

[10]Take, my brethren, the prophets, who have
spoken in the name of the Lord, for an
example of suffering affliction, and of
patience. [11] Behold, we count them happy
which endure. Ye have heard of the patience
of Job, and have seen the end of the Lord; that
the Lord is very pitiful, and of tender mercy.
[12]But above all things, my brethren, swear not,
neither by heaven, neither by earth, neither by
any other oath: but let your yea be yea; and
your nay, nay; lest ye fall into condemnation.

James 5: 10-12

Directions: Respond to the prompts below

1. In suffering are you more likely to get angry with God or seek to understand the greater purpose? Why?

2. What is one of the best lessons you learned after coming through a season of suffering?

Daily Devotional

Job

Suffering does not discriminate. It is experienced by people of all religions, social classes, and ethnicities. Sometimes we suffer as a consequence of our actions. As believers we may suffer as a result of spiritual warfare, the need for development, or even persecution. Some suffering is not the fault of anyone or anything, but comes simply as a result of living in a fallen world.

In the case of Job, a wealthy man who loves the Lord, goes through a series of trials that result in him losing all his possessions, his family, and even his health. At one point his wife tells him to just curse God and die. Job refused. He said that God gives, and God can take away. Blessed be the name of the Lord. At one point he cursed the very day he was born, but would not curse God for his affliction.

Now there is some debate among theologians as to the cause of Job's affliction. Additionally, some believe that the opening dialog between God and Satan did not actually occur, but was rather Job's perception of how he imagined his affliction came to be. Theologians in this camp count chapters 1- 14 to all be Job's story to his friends. Others believe the story unfolded exactly as told.

Regardless of the start, a few things are clear in the story. When God shows up in the whirl wind in chapter 38, he questions Job harshly and demands that Job face up to all the things he had said about God. In chapter 42 Job repents, declaring that he had questioned God's wisdom with ignorance, and spoke of things he knew nothing about. He goes on that up to this point he had only heard of God, but now he could see him. He took back everything he said, and sat in the ashes in his repentance to the Lord.

Job had honored God his entire life. Through his affliction, he remained faithful to God in a way that most of us could not. However, there was a character flaw in him that only affliction could bring to the surface. Two beautiful things came out of this affliction for Job. Not only did it reveal sin he did not know was in his heart, but it also deepened his relationship with God. While he was grumbling to his friends and feeling sorry for himself the foundation was being laid for God to make his presence known in Job's life in a way Job had never experienced it before.

In reading Job's repentance, I sense that the greatest victory for Job that day was not the restoration of his wealth, but rather the reconciliation that took place in his spirit. While Job sat in the ash, I believe the meditation of his heart turned from anguish to gratitude, and his sorrow was exchanged for joy. An encounter with God will do that for you!

Many of the prophets of the Old Testament and early church members faced affliction to the point of Martyrdom, and yet they were blessed. Hebrews 11:36-38 says that by faith they were mocked, beaten, and murdered. In Acts the early church counted it a blessing to be deemed worthy of the persecution of Christ.

There's something about afflictions, regardless of the catalyst, that develops a person and brings them closer to God. There's something about the closeness that gives us joy as we carry on. For that, we are truly a blessed people!

WRAP

Choose a verse from today's reading, and follow the steps below.

Write the verse:	Reflect on its meaning:	Apply it to your life:	Pray about today's reading:

Notes & Questions:

Today's Big Idea

Suffering can bring you closer to God!

Digging Deeper

God is for you

John 3:16 he made a path to salvation
Romans 8:37 he has made us conquerors
Philippians 4:19 he can meet your needs
1 Peter 5:7 he can handle your worries

Getting through Suffering

Isaiah 43:2 God walks through our suffering with us
Romans 5:3 afflictions produce perseverance
Romans 8:35 hardship does not separate us from God
2 Corinthians 1:3-4 God comforts us in our troubles
1 Peter 5:10 you will be established, strengthened, and settled

Day 28

G2553
to suffer evil; endure affliction

G770
To be weak, feeble; weak (physically or morally), sick

G2114
to be of good cheer; keep up spirit, be of good courage

13 Is any among you afflicted? Let him pray. Is
any merry? Let him sing psalms. 14 Is any sick
among you? Let him call for the elders of the
church; and let them pray over him, anointing
him with oil in the name of the Lord: 15 And the
prayer of faith shall save the sick and the Lord
shall raise him up; and if he have committed
sins, they shall be forgiven him. 16A Confess
your faults one to another, and pray one for
another that ye may be healed.

G4982
To save; heal, preserve, rescue

G266
Sin, failure; missing the mark, guilt

James 5: 13-16A

Directions: Respond to the prompts below.

1. What is one piece of encouragement from your victories you could share with someone in an affliction?

2. What is one way that you have seen sin lead to health problems in your life or in the life of others?

Daily Devotional

Today's devotional will be heavy on the commentary and light on stories

Today's reading, instructs us on how we ought to conduct ourselves towards others in life's various seasons. The person living in victory, likely got there by overcoming an affliction. We need their testimony to encourage us. Those that are in affliction, can remind us of the feelings we felt in our valleys so that we avoid pride on our mountain tops. Each person has an experience to share that will benefit the body of Christ. Likewise, each season requires something of the body of Christ. For the afflicted, space to pray without being bombarded by know-it-alls. To the cheerful, the opportunity to glorify God without raining on their parade.

The sick are in need of healing. By the 39 lashes Jesus took, we are healed. Yes, we can use medical intervention, Paul instructed Timothy to use a little wine for his stomach; yes, every man is appointed a time to die; and yes, there is a sickness unto death. But none of us know the days God has numbered for us, so let's not think that it's God's will for us to be sick. Perhaps a season of sickness will double as an affliction, resulting in spiritual development. That doesn't mean that God wants you to stay sick or even that he made you sick. His will is for you to be healed and whole, until the time comes for you to join him in heaven.

When studying the miracles of Jesus and his disciples, the first noteworthy practice is the commitment to prayer in daily life. In Acts, Peter is asked to pray that Dorcas be restored to life, he sought God in prayer first. Elders of the church should be people of prayer, regularly seeking the Lord.

The people who sought Christ for a miracle were desperate for healing. The woman with the issue of blood came to Jesus, after she'd exhausted every option in her power. So, she went to the one with more power than her, and by faith laid aside her pride to grab the hem of his garment.

If you're sick, especially if you've done all that is in your power, seek out the elders at your church to agree with you in prayer for the restoration of your health. Jesus took stripes for your healing; it is not his will for you to remain sick.

Next, James instructs that when praying over the sick they should be anointed with oil. In Mark 6:13 we see that the disciples also anoint the sick with oil. It is most commonly interpreted that the oil is representative of the Holy Spirit, and serves as a reminder that healing does not come from man, but from God.

Finally, James addresses the role of sin in sickness. All sicknesses in the body do not derive from sin. However, sin that is not repented of will cause dis ease in your body and eventually manifest itself as health problems. Jesus said when healing the blind man that his condition was **not** a result of sin in him or his parents. Jesus also told the cripple at the pool of Bethesda to go and sin no more.

To be at our best health, we need to deal with the sin in our hearts, so that it does not manifest into some health condition down the line.

It's easy to get frustrated when healing doesn't come right away, and when there's space between the prayer and the physical healing, but we can rest assured that it is not God's will for us to remain sick, and we can boldly come to him seeking to be healed.

WRAP

Choose a verse from today's reading, and follow the steps below.

Write the verse:	Reflect on its meaning:	Apply it to your life:	Pray about today's reading:

Notes & Questions:

Today's Big Idea

It is the will of God for you to be healthy

Digging Deeper

Overcoming Affliction

Psalms 34:19-20 the Lord delivers us from affliction

2 Corinthians 4:8-12 we will not be destroyed by our hardships

2 Corinthians 6:4-6 our afflictions are a testimony

Praise The Lord

Joshua 6:20 praising God brings down strongholds

2 Chronicles 20:21-22 praising God brings victory

Acts 16:25-26 Praising God brings freedom

Healing

Psalm 147:3 God heals our broken hearts

Isaiah 53:5 Christ suffered for our healing

1 Peter 2:24

Matthew 8:14-17 Jesus bears our sickness

Day 29

G1754
be active, efficient, be mighty; put forth power.

G2480
to be strong, have power; prevail

G3663
of like feelings or affections.

16B The effectual fervent prayer of a righteous man availeth much 17 Elias was a man subject to like passions as we are, and he prayed earnestly that it might not rain: and it rained not on the earth by the space of three years and six months. 18 And he prayed again, and the heaven gave rain and the earth brought forth her fruit.

James 5: 16B-18

Directions: Think of a trial you are currently facing and answer the questions below.

1. What differences did you notice between Elijah's approach to God and the false prophet's approach to Baal?

2. What made Elijah's prayer so effective?

3. What encouragement or challenges can you take from this story?

Daily Devotional

1 Kings 17-19

Under King Ahab places of idol worship were built, prophets of God were killed, and Ahab himself had begun worshipping Baal like his wife Jezebel. God sent Elijah to inform him that rain would not come to Israel until Elijah commanded the rain to return. For the next 3 ½ years no rain would fall in Israel, bringing famine to the land.

When God instructed Elijah to return, he met with Ahab and told him to get together 450 prophets of Baal, 400 prophets of Asherah and all of Israel and meet him at Mount Carmel.

When Elijah arrived at Mount Carmel, he asked everyone, how long they planned to waver between two opinions? Would they worship the God of Israel or Baal? Elijah determined to settle the debate in their minds. He brought out two bulls and told the false prophets that they would get a bull and he would get a bull. They would each dress their bull for sacrifice, and then they would call to their gods, and which ever god lit the fire for the sacrifice would be the true God. The false prophets agreed, and Elijah let them pick their bull first.

The false prophets cried out to their gods until noon with no answer. Elijah mockingly called out to them things like, "call louder, maybe he's talking and can't hear you! Maybe he's left for a journey, or fell asleep" the false prophets pulled out their knives and began cutting themselves before their gods, and still no answer came. This went on through the afternoon.

At the time of the evening sacrifice, Elijah stepped up to prepare his offering. He tore down the wooden altar, and built one of 12 stones for each tribe of Israel. Then he put the wood back in order, and finally prepared the bull and placed it on the altar. Then he had four barrels of water poured on the altar, and filled a trench around the altar with water too. He prayed a simple prayer that the Lord would hear him, and that he would show the people that God was Lord, and turn their hearts back to him. The fire of the Lord fell from heaven and consumed the sacrifice, the wood, the stones, and all of the water from the trench.

As the people of Israel repented, Elijah had all of the false prophets executed. Then he prayed for rain. When the cloud appeared, he sent word to Ahab that he needed to head home, or the rain would hold him up.

Once word reached Jezebel about the state of her prophets, she promised to have Elijah killed before the end of the next day. Elijah was afraid and fled the country and went out to the desert. Once in the desert, he cried out to God that he would just take his life, but God did not answer that prayer in the way Elijah expected. Instead, God gave him rest and sent an angel to nourish him with a cake.

Elijah's close walk with God, positioned him to be a mighty vessel for the Lord. God was able to accomplish great things through Elijah's obedience, and he walked with authority from God. With all this, Elijah was still just like us. Throughout his ministry he encountered moments of fear, depression, loneliness, feeling like he couldn't hear God's voice, and so much more. If God still answered the fervent prayers of Elijah in his weaknesses, imagine what God can do with yours!

WRAP

Choose a verse from today's reading, and follow the steps below.

Write the verse:	Reflect on its meaning:	Apply it to your life:	Pray about today's reading:

Notes & Questions:

Today's Big Idea

Prayer gets things done!

Digging Deeper

When praying for yourself...

Matthew 26:41 pray so that you do not fall into temptation

Philippians 4:6-7 pray about the things that make you anxious

1John 5:14-15 Know that you can confidently ask for anything in accordance with God's will

When praying for others....

Matthew 6:7 pray for those who persecute you

1 John 5:16 pray for those struggling with sin

Ephesians 1:18 pray for their spiritual development

1 Timothy 2:1-2 pray for those in political authority

Day 30

G4105
cause to wonder; lead astray, deceive

G1994
to turn, return, turn back

G2288
Death; physical or spiritual

G2572
To cover; veil, hide, conceal

19 Brethren, if any of you do err from the
truth, and one convert him; 20 Let him know,
that he which converteth the sinner from
the error of his way shall save a soul from
death, and shall hide a multitude of sins.

James 5: 19-20

Directions: Answer the questions below

1. Do you think anybody in the palace could have confronted David with his sin? Why?

2. When it comes to restoring our loved ones to Christ, what is the most important thing for us to do? Why?

3. What behavior would not be helpful in this situation?

Daily Devotional

2 Samuel 12:1-24

After the birth of David's first son with Bathsheba, God sent the prophet Nathan to confront him.

Nathan came to David with a story about two men in a city. The rich man had plenty of cows and sheep, but the poor man had one little ewe lamb. The poor man loved his lamb, having raised her himself in his home with his children. She'd eat his food, and drink out of his cup. When a traveler came to visit the rich man, he didn't want to waste one of his own sheep, so he took the poor man's lamb and prepared her for the traveler to eat.

Being a shepherd in his childhood, David understood the value of a beloved sheep. He was enraged by the rich man who would do such a thing to the beloved sheep of the poor man. He swore that the man who did this thing deserved death. At the very least he would be required to pay back four times the price of the lamb because he did this without any pity.

Nathan said to David, "You are the man!" Nathan went on with his message from the Lord that God had anointed David as king over Israel, rescued him from Saul, given him the houses of Israel and Judah, and if he had wanted more, all he had to do was ask. But in that season, he despised the word of God, doing what was evil. He'd slept with Uriah's wife, then had him killed in battle to cover it up. Then he took her in as his wife.

God promised that because of this sin he would stir up trouble for David within his household, and that the sin of adultery he committed privately, God would see to it that his wives would go to bed with other men openly in front of all of Israel.

David recognized that he had sinned against the Lord, and repented right then and there.

Nathan let him know that The Lord heard David's repentance, and had taken away his sin. David would not die, but since he showed a total contempt for God in his affair, the son that was born would die.

After the death of his son, David returned to worshipping the Lord, and comforted his wife.

David went on in his reign to do many great things for the Lord. David and Bathsheba gave birth to a second son, whom the Lord loved.

Nathan played a vital role in helping restore David's walk with God. Had Nathan been too afraid to confront David, David may have continued down this path into further wickedness. The remaining years of his reign may have looked much different.

In our lives there are times that we see loved ones going down a sinful path. We can take lessons from Nathan on how to approach the ones we love and restore them to Christ. First, Nathan was led of the Lord. Before we confront our loved ones, we need to spend some time in prayer. Second, Nathan opened the conversation with something David could understand. While we're praying about the situation, we should ask God to show us the right way to go about it so that we bring restoration. Third, Nathan did not compromise on the truth when it came to that part of the conversation. Flattery was not going to do David any favors. Finally, he offered David a solution and hope. Let's endeavor to restore our fellow believers by the leading of the Spirit in love!

WRAP

Choose a verse from today's reading, and follow the steps below.

Write the verse:

Reflect on its meaning:

Apply it to your life:

Pray about today's reading:

Notes & Questions:

Digging Deeper

Reconciliation with Christ

John 3:20 we run from the light when we sin due to fear of exposure

Galatians 6:1 those living by the Spirit should help restore a person gently

2 Corinthians 5:17-18 we've been reconciled to God for the ministry of reconciliation (between others and God)

1 John 1:9 we can repent when we've fallen into sin

1 John 5:4 we have victory through Christ to overcome the world

Today's Big Idea

Restoring others to Christ should be motivated by love!

Special Thanks

Thank you to all of the friends and family who helped me through the process of becoming a first-time author. Whether it was teaching me how to self-publish, offering encouragement, proofreading my work, checking my words for Biblical accuracy, or recommending Bible stories for consideration in the devotionals, I thank you!

Made in the USA
Las Vegas, NV
10 August 2022

53056507R00044